Deer-Resistant Gardening in the Midwest: Combined Edition

Sue Monson

Contents

Dedication

To my boyfriend, Ross, for his kind support, and, indirectly, to the deer that keep visiting his backyard, inspiring me to do something about it.

Chapter 1

Introduction

You're sitting on your back porch, enjoying your garden. You put so much time, money, and effort into getting it just right. Now it's a feast for the eyes. Then, you see some deer wander in. They look so serene and gentle, just like Bambi. But wait, they're nibbling on your veggies! You shoo them away, but they come back the next day. Within a week, your hostas are down to the nubs, and some sections of bark are in ribbons from stags rubbing their velvety antlers. What can you do? I am here to answer that question and to give you hope. You can protect your garden from hungry deer and still have a beautiful garden.

Another important incentive to keeping deer out of your yard is the deer ticks that can carry Lyme Disease. You can outsmart them for the most part. First, I must warn you, if deer are hungry enough, they will eat anything. They will go to extreme measures to get at anything resembling food. But they don't like some textures, tastes, and, oddly enough, some colors. Fences will help keep them out, but they are an eyesore. Let's talk about options.

Chapter 2

Physical Protection

If you want to have some plants that deer (and you) consider delicious, you must protect them. A large dog will work as long as he is outside, but deer will see when he is inside. Then the deer will attack their favorite plants. Deer are kinda smart. If you want to have your dog inside at night for personal protection and when the weather gets chilly, you need to consider physical barriers. A fence can also keep a dog with wanderlust or an irresistible curiosity within your yard. Deer can easily jump anything up to seven feet high if they can see a nice landing area. If you bury a fence a foot and a half into the ground, you can prevent burrowing creatures from entering as well. Bear in mind that this means the total height of your fence will now be nine and a half feet. If a fence is your choice, anything less than eight feet means you must do something else.

Deer will not jump a fence if they can't see a safe landing spot, so two fences six feet tall and four feet apart will keep the deer away, but they make your yard look like a battleground. I suppose it is a battleground but who wants that look?

If you have tasty seedlings that you may have started inside, you can put a shorter fence around them and make a section of extra fencing into a roof. This roof means you can't weed them unless you have an easy way to remove the roof, so lay a ground cover before planting.

Another option is to electrify the fence. Deer will keep testing it, so don't turn it off for any length of time. Be sure to check local ordinances before installing any fence, especially an electric fence.

Putting fishing lines around the garden will help deter deer, as they can't see it after dark. The lines might be a good option paired with a dog who is outside during the day. An invisible fence can keep the dog inside the yard.

If you need to protect your young trees from damage caused by deer rubbing their antlers against the bark, you can erect a fence around the tree. Chicken wire is good enough here. Just wrap it around.

You can tell what animal is damaging your tree by looking at the marks. Of course, rabbit and rodent marks are lower than deer marks. Torn jagged looking tears in the bark are from deer. Deer have no upper incisors, so they must grab and tear. Squirrels and rabbits leave a clean-cut mark about 45 degrees from vertical. Rabbit marks are usually the width of a spoon, whereas rodent marks look like they were made with a fork. All can cause permanent damage to expensive trees.

It goes without saying (oops, I said it) that you must keep these fences in good repair. Deer constantly check their boundaries, just like children. Make sure your metal fencing is galvanized and your propy-lene fencing is UV-protected to ensure a long-lasting barrier. Black coated wire mesh fencing is almost invisible in the yard. Make sure your fencing is rated for more than eight hundred pounds breaking load. Deer are strong. Wooden privacy fences are an option if they are tall enough to prevent deer from seeing the other side. The gate will need to be deer proof as well. A greenhouse is always an option.

Chapter 3

Chemical Repellant

You can utilize chemical deer repellants if you don't want to look at a fence but still want your tasty veggies. You can purchase deer repellant spray, which must be applied repeatedly, as the rain will wash it off. One which is supposed to be good is called Liquid Fence Deer and Rabbit Repellant. If you want to make one yourself, you'll need something that smells like a predator- a wolf maybe. Hunting stores can usually supply what you need.

Chapter 4

Deer-Resistant Plants

The easiest option is to plant stuff that deer don't especially like. Anything with a strong flavor, like onions or garlic, or a strong odor, like marigolds, will encourage deer to try next door instead. Furry or spiky leaves irritate their sensitive noses, as will thorns. Deer don't like gray-colored leaves. Using deer-resistant plants around the garden perimeter will discourage deer from tasting more desirable plants farther in. Deer are creatures of habit, and they will remember the best plants from last year and hit them again. They will also remember the location of plants they dislike.

Set realistic goals when it comes to deer damage. A 50% reduction in damage is great, but 30% is average. Deer can jump up to twelve feet in the air and squeeze through gaps as small as seven and a half inches if they are highly motivated, i.e. running for their lives.

Here in the Midwest, we get large ranges of temperatures from season to season. We are in Zones 3-8. The Zone is determined by how cold it gets in the winter. Be aware of how hot it gets in the summer too. When I lived in Minnesota, I was amazed that a place that got sooooo cold in the winter could get so hot and humid in the summer. When I lived in Upstate New York (yes, I moved around a lot) it didn't get as cold in the winter or as hot in the summer.

When going through the list, note that some sub-species are deer resistant, while other subspecies are not. My boyfriend had one sub-species of hostas completely eaten down to the ground, and another subspecies wasn't touched. If you see an "sp" after the species name, that means that all the subspecies I saw are deer-resistant. When in doubt, ask your local garden center specialist for advice. When available, I put the Rutgers rating down. "A" means the plant is rarely damaged by deer, "B" means it is seldom severely damaged. I didn't bother to put anything in category C or D into the table since those are not deer-resistant.

Did you know that deer eat different plants at different times of the year? In the early spring, especially if there is deep snow, deer are hungry and will eat anything. They love the tasty young green shoots, as they get a third of their water from moist, tender plants such as lettuce and beans. In late summer and fall, deer eat acorn mast to store fat for the winter. Deer are creatures of habit, and they will remember the best plants from last year and hit them again, each and every year.

Chapter 5

Images and Descriptions of Deer-Resistant Plants

Abelia, Glossy (abelia x grandiflora) (a-BEE-lee-uh ex gran-dih-FLOR-uh)

Glossy Abelia is a rounded, spreading, multi-stemmed shrub in the Honeysuckle family. It grows on gracefully arching branches from two to four feet tall. If the stems die to the ground in a harsh winter, the plant survives. Flowering will still occur, but only bloom on smaller plants that reach a height of a foot to a foot and a half. Clusters of fragrant, white-tinged, bell-shaped flowers appear over a long bloom period - late spring to fall. Glossy, dark green leaves turn purplish-bronze in autumn. Easily grown in average, medium, well-drained soil in full sun to partial shade in Zones 6-9. Best flowering is in full sun. Prefers moist, organically rich soils that drain well. Somewhat evergreen in the South, but generally deciduous in the Midwest, stems may suffer substantial damage (including dying to the ground) in cold winters. Significant stem damage can be expected when winter temperatures approach zero degrees F. Best suited to a protected location. Blooms on new wood, so prune as needed (e.g., remove stems lost to winter and, if desired, cut to the ground) in late winter to early spring. Rutgers rating B.

Aconite, Winter (eranthis hyemalis) (ee-RAN-this ky-EH-may-liss)

Winter Aconite is best grown in organically rich, medium moisture, well-drained soils in full sun to partial shade. It's best planted under deciduous trees to enjoy the full sun at the time of bloom, but acquire increasing shade as overhead trees leaf out. This plant needs consistent moisture year-round (albeit less in summer and fall) even though the plant goes dormant by late spring. It may self-seed and naturalize over time in optimum growing conditions. However, it's best left undisturbed once planted. One of the first signs of spring, this rugged plant often sends it's shoots up through the snow. Green leaves emerge after the flowers. Max height is one foot, Zones 3-7, full sun, yellow flowers in the early spring. Rutgers rating A. Some sources suggest Aconite to help pain, fright, fever, or restlessness.

Ageratum (Ageratum houstonianum)   (a-jer-AY-tum hoos-tone-ee-AY-num)

Easily grown in average, moist, well-drained soils in full sun, Ageratum prefers rich soils with good drainage and consistent moisture throughout the growing season. Plants tend to wilt quickly if the soil is allowed to dry out. Tolerates light shade. Plants may bloom to frost, and the first autumn frost will kill most if not all plants. Watch for aphids and whiteflies. Taller plants usually benefit from some support. Leaves are hairy, which deer do not like. Max height two feet, Zones 2-10, full sun or partial sun, purple flowers from spring through fall. Rutgers rating A.

Allium (allium) (AL-ee-um)

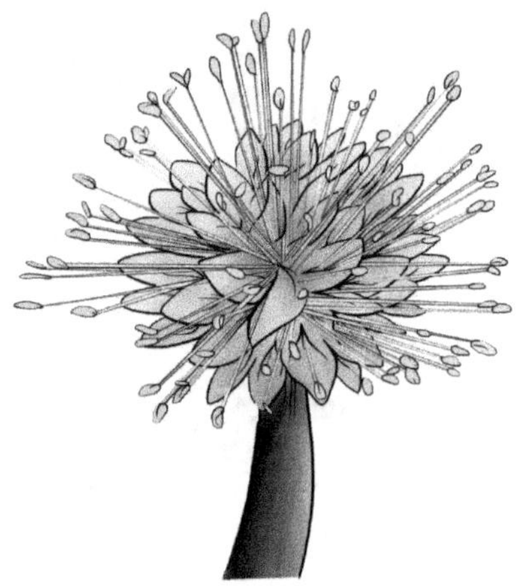

Anything in the Allium family is an onion with the odor and taste that go along with all onions. Deer do not like strong odors and tastes so will generally leave this alone. Bulb rot may occur in overly moist soils. Slugs can attack young plants. Mildew, rust, and leaf spots may appear. Watch for onion maggots and thrips (tiny insects with fringed wings). Bulbs are winter hardy only to Zone 5 or 6, so Midwesteners need to bring them in over the winter. Max height eight feet, Zones 4-9, full sun or partial sun, yellow-green blooms in spring through fall. Some herbal references cite Allium to relieve cold symptoms.

Allspice, Carolina (calycanthus floridus) (kal-ee-KAN-thus FLOR-id-us)

Carolina Allspice are dense, rounded deciduous shrubs with a habit of spreading by sending out suckers. They grow six to nine feet (less frequently to twelve feet) tall with an equal or slightly greater spre ad.They feature very fragrant brown to reddish-brown flowers (two inches across) that bloom at the ends of short branchlets in May. Be sure to buy these when they are blooming, as the quality and quantity of scent vary from plant to plant. Some people describe the scent as a mix of Pineapple, Strawberry, and Banana. Even the leaves are fragrant when bruised. If the fragrance isn't enough to repel the deer, who don't like strong scents, the leaves are hairy as well. Traditional medicine suggests Allspice can help indigestion.

Amaranth (AM-ahr-anth), Globe (gomphrena globosa) (gom-FREE-nah glo-BO-sah)

The flowers on a Common Globe Amaranth are insignificant, tiny, white to yellow trumpets only visible close-up. The bright magenta bracts arranged in globe-like, papery flower heads provide the real show in a long summer to frost bloom. They are drought-resistant but grow better with regular watering. They are also very heat tolerant. If you're growing from seed, be generous as the germination rate is low. Max height eight feet, Zones 2-11, full sun needed.

Amsonia, Blue Star (amsonia tabernaemontana) (am-SO-nee-uh tab-er-nay-mon-TAY-nuh)

Blue Star Amsonia is drought-resistant and prefers well-drained soil. It can even tolerate clay soil. When grown in full sun, plants do not require staking, but they become more floppy in shady areas, requiring staking. Max height three feet, Zones 3-9, full sun or partial sun, blue flowers in spring.

Angelica   (angelica   atropurpurea)   (an-JEL-ih-kah
at-re-pur-PURR-ee-uh)

Purple-stemmed Angelica, sometimes called Masterwort, is a large
perennial which can get to ten feet high under optimum conditions.
Native to stream banks and swampy areas in Canada and the Midwest,
Native Americans used the young stems and leaf stalks as cooked
vegetables. Grows in full sun to partial sun in medium to wet soil
in Zones 4-7. The white to greenish-white flowers last from June to
September.

Aster, False (boltonia astroides) (bol-TONE-ee-ah ass-ter-OY-deez)

False Asters can be grown in well-drained soil with full sun for best results. It tolerates relatively dry soils well. If they don't get enough sun or get too much water, they may flop over and require support. They spread, so keep a close eye on them. Max height eight feet, Zones 4-9, white, pink, or lilac flowers in the summer and fall, Rutgers rating B.

Aster, Stokes' (STOHKS) (stokesia laevis) (sto-KEE-see-ah LAY-viss)

Stokes' Aster is native to the southeastern United States and can grow in Zones 5-9. Wet soil in winter is the chief cause of death for these plants, so make sure your soil is well-drained. It prefers moist, sandy soils but can tolerate drought and heat. Deadhead blooms to encourage reblooming. Max height three feet, Zones 5-9, full sun or partial sun, purplish-blue flowers in summer and fall, rabbit-resistant, Rutgers rating B.

Astilbe (astilbe) (ah-STILL-bee)

Astilbes are best grown in average, medium moisture, well-drained soils in partial shade to full shade. Do not allow the soil to dry out. Many gardeners leave the blooms after they dry out because of the aesthetic appeal of the dried seed heads. Divide the clumps every 3-4 years to avoid overcrowding. Powdery mildew and wilt may appear. Japanese beetles may chew on the foliage. Excellent ground cover or edging plant for shady areas. Max height three feet, Zones 4-8, full sun or partial sun, rabbit-resistant,. Purple, red, white, or pink flowers arrive in spring and summer.

Avens (geum sp) (JEE-um)

Avens can be used as ground covers around yards and driveways, but make sure your soil is well-drained, or they won't last the winter. After flowering, they form fluffy seed pods, so you can deadhead some blooms to encourage reblooms, but don't do all of them, or you won't have any seed pods to look at during the winter. They enjoy full sun, but a little shade during long hot summers would be welcome. Max height three feet, Zones 3-9, various colors depending on the variety during the summer.

Barberry (berberis) (BUR-bur-is)

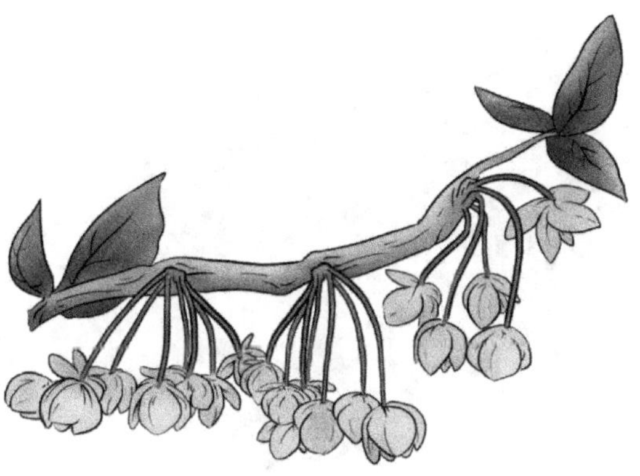

Japanese Barberry, also called Oregon Grape-Holly (mahonia japonica), is considered invasive in the Midwest, but other varieties of Barberry (berberis) are ok to use. Max height eight feet, Zones 3-9, full sun or partial sun, yellow flowers that bloom in the spring, Rutgers rating A. Some Barberry varieties might not be deer-tolerant, so make sure before buying, as there are 400 varieties. Buy two plants so they can pollinate and produce berries. All Barberry varieties feature spiny stems which bother deer. Some sources suggest Barberry bark is useful for urinary tract infection pain as it contains the alkaloid berberine.

Barrenwort (epimedium x perralchicum) (ep-ih-MEE-dee-um pair-AL-chee-kum)

Barrenwort is a ground cover with waxy textured flowers and can tolerate drought once established. It needs to be in an area protected from cold, dry winds in the winter or you will have to prune it severely in the spring. It likes partial sun or shade and loosely packed soil. Zones 4-8, rabbit-resistant, Rutgers rating A and yellow flowers that bloom in the spring.

Basil (ocimum basilicum) (OH-sih-mum ex bass-IL-ee-kum)

Basil is a native of Africa and Asia. Traditions say basil was found growing around Christ's tomb after the Resurrection. Some Greek Orthodox churches use it to prepare holy water and pots of basil are set below church altars. In India, basil was believed to be imbued with divine essence, and oaths were sworn upon it in courts.

Many varieties exist today, ranging from tiny-leafed Greek basil to robust two-foot-high plants with large succulent leaves. Some varieties have deep purple leaves. While flowers are typically small and whitish; some can be pink to brilliant magenta. Leaves can be dried for later use in cooking. Basil is extremely frost-sensitive. Sow seeds in early spring. Grows best in full sun in moderately rich and well-drained soil that is kept well watered. Pinch out centers to encourage bushy growth. As frost approaches, root cuttings in water and pot for winter use. Zones 2-11, full sun or partial sun, rabbit-resistant, blooms summer through fall.

Basket of Gold (aurinia saxatilis) (aw-RIN-ee-uh sak-A-til-iss)

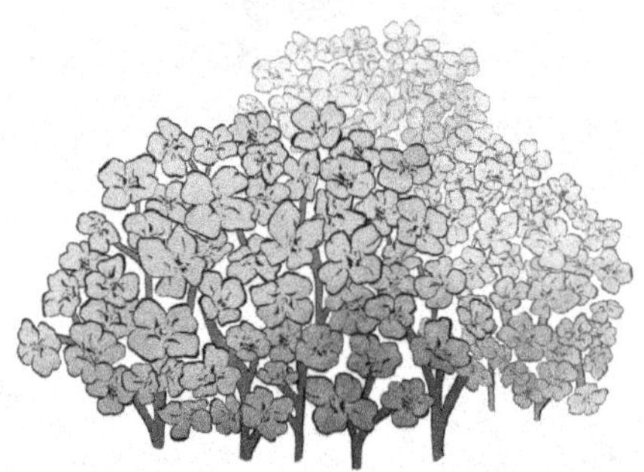

Basket of Gold grows in dry, average to sandy, well-drained soils in full sun. Avoid heavy clay soils. Root rot may develop in moist or poorly-drained soils. The best flowering is in full sun. Leaves are gray-green, which may be why deer avoid them. As mentioned before, deer dislike gray foliage for some unknown reason. Max height three feet, full sun needed, Zones 3-7, Rutgers A rating, yellow flowers in spring.

Bayberry, Northern (myrica pensylvanica) (MIR-i-ka pen-sill-VAN-ee-ka)

Northern Bayberry is a dense shrub that tolerates salty conditions well, like seashores and along roads. If you want berries, plant a male shrub beside as many female shrubs as you want. The berries are coated with a waxy substance that is used to make candles. The wax and the grayish-green leaves both contribute to its deer resistance, as well as the fact that the leaves are aromatic when crushed. Max height twenty feet, Zones 3-7, full sun or partial sun, Rutgers rating A, yellowish-green flowers in the spring only on male plants.

Beautyberry (callicarpa) (kal-ee-KAR-puh)

Beautyberry plants prefer soil like native forest floors- moist clay or sand with lots of organic matter. It fruits best in full sun but will survive partial sun with less fruit. Even if the winter kills the part of the plant which is above ground, it will come back in the spring and still bear fruit. Zones 5-8, Rutgers rating B, purple or pink flowers in spring and summer.

Bee Balm (monarda didyma) (mo-NAR-da DID-ee-muh)

Bee Balm, also called Wild Bergamot or Oswego Tea, is named for its plant resin use in reducing inflammation from bee stings. The Oswego Indians of Upstate New York steeped the leaves in tea. You can do the same, and also use the leaves in salads. Leaves emit a minty fragrance when bruised, which deer don't particularly like. It is rabbit-resistant as well. The plant can suffer from mildew, especially in a crowded clump where air circulation is low. Deadhead blooms and do not allow the soil to dry out. Max height eight feet, Zones 3-9, full sun, red flowers in the summer/fall. Rutgers rating B.

Beech,   American   (fagus   grandifoia)   (FAG-us
grand-dih-FOH-lee-uh)

The American Beech tree is native to eastern North America and
is known for its smooth grayish bark. The tree is oval shaped and can
reach fifty feet high and forty feet wide. It likes moist, well-drained soil
best, and will not do well in wet or poorly-drained soil. It is difficult to
transplant and doesn't do well in urban settings. The ovate to elliptical
leaves turn golden bronze in the fall. In late spring, greenish flowers
appear in drooping clusters on males and short spikes on females. The
female blooms ripen into triangular edible nuts. It prefers Zones 3-9
and full sun to part shade.

Begonia, Wax (begonia semperflorens)) (bah-GO-nee-ah sem-per-VEER-enz)

Wax Begonias are not winter-hardy in the Midwest, so you should plant them as annuals every year. They are good as edgers or in flower boxes or other containers. If in containers, you can bring them inside in the fall into a cool area of the house, do not water them much, and they just might flourish again in the spring. Plant outside after the last spring frost. They tolerate full sun, partial sun, or shade, but will flower less in shade. Max height two feet, Zones 7-11 but can tolerate more northerly Zones if you bring them in for the winter. Their waxy leaves make them drought-tolerant but also make them less appetizing to deer. The flowers are in various shades of pink and white, and bloom throughout the growing season. Space them well apart to avoid fungal problems.

Bellflower (campanula sp) (kam-PAN-yoo-luh)

Clustered Bellflowers love the full sun in northern areas but need partial sun in southern areas of the Midwest. The pink and lavender flowers may rebloom if you deadhead them. Hummingbirds and butterflies are attracted to this plant. Divide them every few years, especially in moist soils. Max height three feet, Zones 3-9.

Birch (betula) (BET-yoo-luh)

The grayish-white bark of Birch trees reminds me of northern Michigan, where my mom grew up. They prefer snow in winter, moist, acidic, sandy, or rocky soils. Use a soaker hose if you are far enough south to reach above 75 deg F in the summer, which covers most of the Midwest. You can also use mulch to keep the moisture from evaporating. It can reach twenty feet in height and usually does not require pruning. Yellow-green flowers appear in the spring. Zones 3-7, full sun or partial sun.

Black-eyed Susan (rudbeckia sp) (rud-BEK-ee-ah)

Black-eyed Susans are a familiar plant to us Midwesterners. They tolerate hot, humid summers and thrive in full sun. They can tolerate some drought once established. Divide clumps every five years to encourage growth and deadhead blooms to encourage a long blooming season. Flowers have yellow petals with black centers and serve as a nice accent in cut flower arrangements. Watch for aphids, mildew, and septoria leaf spot, as well as Asters' yellow disease. Max height three feet, Zones 3-7, blooms summer through fall. Butterflies love them.

Bleeding Heart (dicentra sp) (dy-SEN-truh)

I love Bleeding Heart plants. They look so cool in hanging baskets with their blooms hanging down below the level of the basket. They don't like their soil getting too dry in the summer or too wet in the winter. If planted in the ground, good soil drainage is essential for their survival. Rutgers rating A. They can tolerate full sun or partial sun in Zones 3-7. Max height three feet. The flowers will bloom from spring through fall if you keep the plant happy. Rabbit-resistant as well. Grayish-green leaves may provide a clue to their deer resistance.

Bloodroot (sanguinaria canadensis) (SAN-gwin-AH-ree-ah kan-ah-DEN-sis)

Bloodroot is a native Midwestern wildflower that Native Americans used for dye. The rootstock is poisonous but can be used for antiseptic and emetic purposes. The sap, flowing whenever the plant is cut, is bright orange-red, which explains the name. Flowers close up at night and only last a day or two. They spread in the wild throughout the forest floor, never getting more than a foot tall. White or pink-tinged flowers appear in the spring. They prefer full shade but can tolerate partial sun. Zones 3-8.

Bluebeard (caryopteris clandonensis) (kar-ee-OP-ter-iss klan-don-EN-sis)

Bluebeard, also called Blue Spirea (spy-REE-ah) or Blue Mist, is a low, mounded shrub that has aromatic leaves when touched and blue flowers that bloom in the late summer and resemble blue clouds. They will need to be pruned hard after the winter, and the flowers bloom on new growth, so don't worry. Flowers are attractive to bees, butterflies, and other beneficial insects. Max height eight feet, Zones 4-8, full sun, drought-tolerant.

Bluebell, Virginia (mertensia virginica) (mer-TEN-saa-uh vir-JIN-ih-kuh)

Virginia Bluebells are a native Midwestern plant that grows in rich woods and river floodplains. It thrives in partial sun and shade. The blue flowers arrive in early spring, having pinkish buds that gradually turn blue. Foliage dies to the ground by mid-summer, when the plant goes dormant, so it won't look pretty without another plant to pick up the slack in your garden. Max height three feet, Zones 3-8, Rutgers rating B.

Bluestem, Little (schizachyrium scoparium) (ski-za-KRY-ee-um sko-PAIR-ee-um)

Little Bluestem is a forgiving ornamental grass. You can flood it, dry it out, offer it no shade, high heat, and humidity, shallow or rocky soil, and still, it keeps growing like a trooper. It needs to be cut back to the ground in late winter or early spring. In the fall, the leaves turn bronze and the purplish-bronze flowers appear above the leaves. Each leaf has a bluish tinge at the base, which accounts for the name. Max height four feet, Zones 3-8, full sun, drought-tolerant once established.

Borage (borago officinalis) (bor-AY-go oh-fi-shi-NAH-lis)

Borage is a plant native to the Mediterranean area but will do well in Zones 3-11. The blue flowers come in summer with wrinkled, hairy gray-green leaves. These leaves aren't very appealing to deer, as they dislike the gray color and hairy leaves. For us, the leaves are edible and can be prepared like spinach when tender and young. They are said to smell and taste a bit like cucumber. They can reach three feet tall and do well in full sun or partial sun. Rutgers rating B.

Boxwood, Common (buxus sempervirens) (BUK-sus sem-per-VY-renz)

Boxwood is a great choice for a hedge between properties, but make sure it has some shade and is protected from the wind. Otherwise, it will turn bronze, which isn't very pretty. The flowers are insignificant, so don't count on them brightening up the green leaves. Prune them after the last frost to allow air circulation, thus avoiding pests. They can reach thirty feet high if left alone, but pruning is recommended to prevent them from looking scraggly. Zones 4-8 or 5-8, depending on the source. Rutgers rating A, and rabbit-resistant as well. They prefer partial sun but will tolerate shade if you don't mind an airier bush.

Brunnera, Heartleaf (brunnera macrophylla) (BROO-ner-uh mak-roh-FIL-uh)

Heartleaf Brunnera is sometimes called Siberian Bugloss, which doesn't mean it never has a bug problem, although that is usually the case. It comes from a Greek word meaning ox tongue, referring to the shape of the leaves. The flowers rise above the shrub in the spring and look like forget-me-nots with a white center. This plant will slowly spread. It prefers cool summers and may scorch in the summer sun. It prefers shade but will tolerate partial sun. Rabbit-resistant. Max height three feet, Zones 3-8.

Bugbane (actaea simplex) (ak-TEE-uh SIM-plecks)

Bugbane is another plant with an odd name. This time it is well deserved. The strong odor does repel insects. It is also called Cohosh from an Algonquin word meaning rough, referring to the blooms. This odor is why it repels deer as well. It prefers full shade or at least partial shade and likes moist soil. It dries out easily and can scorch in the sun. It performs best when sheltered from the wind. It is slow to establish so be patient with this one. The white spiky flowers show up in late summer, and the plant can reach four feet high, eventually. Zones 4-9.

Bunchberry (cornus canadensis) (KOR-muhs kan-ah-DEN-sis)

Bunchberry deserves its name. The berries that arrive in the fall after the white flowers fade, truly are in bunches. They are edible as well. It is native to northern North America and eastern Asia, making it one of the few circumpolar plants. It prefers full shade and works well under trees as a ground cover. It does not tolerate foot traffic, so look but don't walk. The leaves turn reddish-purple in the fall. It is rabbit-resistant and deer-resistant, making it ideal for a yard with lots of four-legged visitors. Max height one foot, Zones 2-6.

Bush, Butterfly (buddleia) (BUD-lee-uh)

The Butterfly Bush is heaven to butterflies and bees, but be careful or it will take over the place. It spreads by self-seeding, so gather the seed pods before they split open and disperse their seeds. It has been declared invasive in some states, but not in the Midwest. Prune it down to the ground in late fall. It loves full sun but will tolerate partial sun if you don't expect too much of it. It doesn't like wet feet so make sure the soil is well-draining. Purple or pink flowers bloom in the summer, depending on the particular cultivar. It is rabbit-resistant and can reach fifteen feet tall and fifteen feet wide, with showy flowers arching over the leaves. Zones 5-10, Rutgers rating A.

Bush, Lily of the Valley (pieris japonica) (pee-AIR-iss juh-PON-ih-kuh)

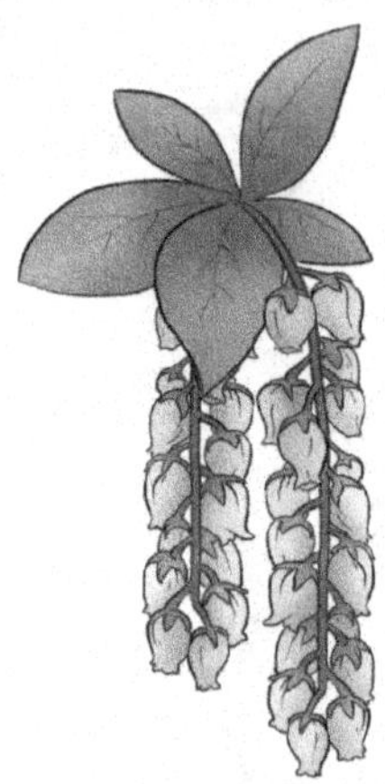

The Lily of the Valley Bush (pieris japonica) is not the same as the Lily of the Valley (convallaria majus). This bush originated in Japan and eastern China and can also be called Japanese Pieris. It grows best when sheltered from the afternoon sun and the wind. Flower buds are set in late summer for the following year, so prune this one directly after blooming or not at all. Keep an eye out for lace bug infestations. It can reach twelve feet tall and eight feet wide in ideal conditions. The white flowers droop in clusters in the spring. Remove spent flowers immediately to make room for those buds for next year. Zones 5-8. Leaves and flowers are poisonous upon ingestion.

Bush, Spice (lindera benzoin) (lin-DEER-ruh ben-ZOH-in)

The Spice Bush is native to the Midwest and shows off in the fall when the leaves turn gold. It can grow up to twelve feet tall and twelve feet wide if left alone. If you want berries, make sure to have both male and female plants. Leaves are aromatic when crushed, which is why deer don't like this particular plant. The larva (caterpillar stage) of the Spice Bush Swallowtail Butterfly feeds on the leaves of this bush. This plant can tolerate full shade, but it will be more open in structure. Fall color is better when in full sun. The spring flowers are greenish-yellow. Zones 4-9.

Butterfly   Weed   (asclepias   tuberosa)   (ass-KLE-pee-us
too-ber-OH-suh)

The Butterfly Weed does well in poor, dry soils and can be grown
from seed. It is slow to establish and should not be moved once it
has grown its large taproot into the soil. It may take two to three
years for flowers to appear, but they are showy, orange-red clusters of
blooms once they come. It can spread by self-seeding if the seed pods
are not removed before they split open. Those pods are used in dried
flower arrangements. The flowers feed many butterflies, and the leaves
feed the larvae of monarch butterflies. It is also called pleurisy root,
referencing old medicinal use of the roots to treat lung inflammation.
It needs full sun and can reach three feet in height and as much in
breadth. Zones 5-10. Drought-tolerant and can grow in rocky soil.
Rutgers rating B.

Camas, Large (camassia leichtlinii) (kuh-MAS-ee-uh leekt-LIN-ee-eye)

The Large Camas plant produces white, cream, blue, and purple blooms, depending on the plant. They last from spring through summer but don't show up until the third or fourth year if grown from seed. It will tolerate dry conditions after the flowers are gone. It is native to the western US. The name comes from the word kamas or quamash from Native American use of the bulb for food. It can grow to four feet tall and two feet wide. Zones 4-8, Rutgers rating B.

Camomile, German (matricaria recutita) (ah-tri-CAR-ee-ah re-KOO-tee-ta)

German Chamomile flowers are in the familiar relaxing teas. These leaves are less bitter than those of Roman Chamomile. It originated in Europe and eastern Asia, was taken to American gardens, and self-seeded its way out of the gardens and into the wild. The fragrant leaves and flowers explain the plant's deer resistance. It prefers full sun but can tolerate partial sun. Zones 2-8, Rutgers rating A. White flowers with yellow centers arrive in the spring and last until fall. Plants reach two feet in height and one foot across. Flower petals can be used for teas fresh or dried. Freeze for later use if desired.

Candytuft (iberis sempervirens) (eye-BEER-is sem-per-VY-renz)

Candytuft is a low evergreen shrub that requires full sun and good drainage. It is drought-tolerant but will develop problems if the roots stay wet. Mulch the plant in winter to avoid sun scorching and desiccation. Cut back about a third after flowering to keep it compact and encourage new growth. The white flowers may cover all the leaves, fading gradually to light pink. Plants reach about a foot high and a foot and a half wide. They spread by stems rooting where they touch the ground. Rabbit-resistant. Zones 3-8, Rutgers rating B.

Catmint (nepeta x faassenii) (NEP-eh-tah fah-SEEN-ee-eye)

Catmint is tolerant of dry soil and even drought. Its grayish-green leaves and bluish-purple flowers are both very aromatic, so deer avoid them. Cut flower spikes after initial flowering to promote more blooms. It forms a spreading clump, reaching two feet high and three feet wide. Zones 3-8.

Catnip (nepeta cataria) (NEP-eh-tah kat-AR-ee-uh)

Catnip is familiar to all because of the effect it has on cats. They love the stuff. What you may not know is it can spread to the point of becoming invasive. It likes full sun or partial sun and can reach three feet high and three feet wide. It can tolerate dry soil and even rocky soil. The fragrance of the leaves may drive deer away, even as it attracts cats and butterflies, although probably not at the same time. White flowers with pale purple spotting arrive in the summer. Zones 3-9.

Cedar, Red Eastern (juniperus virginiana) (jew-NIP-er-us vir-jin-ee-AN-uh)

The Eastern Red Cedar tolerates a wide range of soil conditions but doesn't like having wet feet constantly. It has the best drought resistance of any conifer native to the eastern US. It has gray to reddish-brown bark that can peel off in mature trees. Heartwood is reddish-brown and commonly used for cedar chests. Dark bluish-green scale-like foliage can turn brownish-green in the winter. The female trees produce small round berry-like cones which attract birds. Plant male and female trees together for best results. Avoid planting near Apple trees as Cedar Apple rust is common. This dense tree can grow to seventy-five feet tall and is tolerant of heat, drought, salt, and cold. Zones 2-9. Rutgers rating B.

Cherry, Flowering, Japanese (prunus serrulata) (PROO-nus ser-yoo-LAY-tuh)

The Japanese Flowering Cherry Tree is a familiar sight in the spring in Japan and Washington, DC, but will grow anywhere in Zones 5-8 if it has full sun. The white to pink flowers are beautiful and cover the entire tree in the spring. The cherries come later and are tasty. The tree can reach twenty-five feet tall and just as wide, can tolerate a little shade but loves the sun. It is susceptible to many insect and disease pests, so be aware. Rutgers rating B.

Chestnut, American (castanea dentata) (kas-TAN-nee-uh den-TAY-tuh)

The American Chestnut tree grows best in Zones 5-8 to a height of fifty feet and a spread just as impressive. The yellow-white blooms arrive in June, larger in male blooms but not very impressive anywhere. It prefers full sun and medium moisture soil. This is a high-maintenance tree as it's prone to blight. There is ongoing research into blight-resistant varieties, but the blight has decimated the entire American population. Small nuts are sweet and edible but are encased in spiny burrs.

Chives, Garlic (allium tuberosum) (AL-ee-um too-ber-OH-sum)

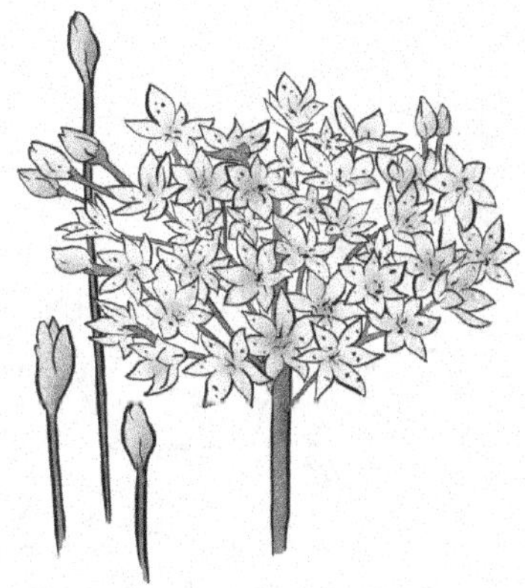

Garlic Chives, as you might suspect, are way too aromatic for deer to tolerate. It can reach three feet tall, loves the sun, and is found in Zones 3-9. It is native to eastern Asia. It spreads aggressively, so be sure to deadhead the flowers before the seed pods open and disperse their seeds all over the place. Its grayish-green leaves can be cooked in the same manner as green onions. The scent of the creamy-white flower, surprisingly, is like that of violets.

Chokecherry, Red (aronia arbutifolia) (ar-ROH-nee-uh ar-bew-tih-FOH-lee-uh)

The Red Chokecherry gets its name from its berries being so astringent that anyone who tries to eat one will choke. The berries do make a tasty jam, however. It can tolerate wet, boggy soil, making it ideal for along river beds. It does spread rapidly, so watch it. It will grow to ten feet tall and six feet wide. The white to light pink flowers appear in spring, followed by red fruits. The leaves turn bright red in the fall, rivaling the Burning Bush for fall color. It can tolerate partial sun but does best in full sun. Zones 4-9. Rutgers rating B.

Cicely, Sweet (myrrhis odorata) (MIR-iss oh-dor-AH-tuh)

Sweet Cicely is an herb that resembles a fern. It originated in western and central Europe, where it has naturalized and spread all over. It came to America with settlers because of its ability to aid digestion. It is rarely used in herb gardens today. Best if grown in light or full shade, it can tolerate full sun if kept well watered. If in a container, plant it in a deep pot to accommodate the deep taproot. It will self-seed in a garden, growing to four feet in height and smelling of licorice and aniseed. Tiny white flowers in the early spring turn into small ribbed fruits with only ornamental interest. Dark brown, licorice-flavored seeds emerge in the early fall. It is also known as Sweet Chervil or Myrrh, but should not be confused with the Myrrh we've all heard about in Christmas tales. Zones 3-9.

Cinquefoil (SINK-foyl) (potentilla sp) (poh-ten-TILL-uh)

The Cinquefoil plant will tolerate light shade but not full shade, preferring full sun. It forms a mound five inches high and spreads to a foot wide. Established plants have good drought tolerance. Excellent winter hardiness. Zone 2-7, Rutgers rating A. White blooms in the spring with a more modest showing in the fall.

Clematis (clematis sp) (KLEM-ah-tis)

Clematis is a genus of over 250 species, all of which sport fragrant blooms from spring to fall. The vines need support but can reach about six feet tall and four feet wide. The flowers like full sun or partial sun, but the soil under the plant requires shade. You can even plant a ground cover over the established roots to ensure shade. The flower color varies by species, with purple being the favorite. Zones 4-9. The aroma of the flowers is definitely what is keeping the deer away.

Clover, Purple Prairie (dalea purpurea) (DAY-lee-uh per-per-EE-ah)

The Purple Prairie Clover is native to North America. Its deep taproot enables it to withstand drought conditions once the plant is established. The purple blooms are on a cone-shaped plant, giving it an odd appearance. The cone part is prickly, giving the deer a hard time. Its aroma attracts butterflies, also repelling the deer. It needs full sun. Zones 3-8. Max height three feet. Commonly used in prairie restorations.

Coleus   (KOE-lee-uss)   (solenostemon   hybrids) (sol-en-oh-STEM-on)

Coleus plants are common indoor plants. I have one myself. They do well outside in Zones 2-11, from full sun to partial sun to shade. They get more colorful in full sun. They grow up to eight feet tall. The variety you choose determines its light requirements and coloring. You can bring it indoors for the winter if you wish.

Columbine (aquilegia canadensis) (ak-will-EE-zsee-eye kan-ah-DEN-sis)

Columbine plants are perennials with a variety of flower colors and are generally winter hardy. The flowers are short-lived but the plant will self-seed. It likes partial sun and needs moist, well-drained soil. Rutgers rating B, Zones 3-9. Hummingbirds love the bell-shaped flowers, which bloom in the spring through the summer. Deer and rabbits would rather leave it alone. It can reach three feet in height.

Comfrey (symphytum x rubrum) (sim-FY-tuhm ROO-brum)

Comfrey is a plant used for ages for its medicinal value when applied to wounds as a poultice. Able to grow in Zones 4-9 to a max height of three feet, it can abide full sun or partial sun. Flower color varies from blue to purple to white, blooming in late spring. It can spread aggressively by creeping rhizomes, even from a tiny bit left in the soil. It is drought-resistant.

Coneflower   (echinacea   purpurea)   (eh-kih-NAY-shah
per-per-EE-ah)

Purple Coneflower, sometimes known by its Latin name Echinacea
Purpurea, is common in the Midwest. Its extract is seen in capsule
form in the herbal supplements aisle in the drug store, and is used to
prevent colds. I've tried it myself but can't tell if it prevented colds or
not. The plant is a perennial and should be split every five years. It is
tolerant of drought, heat, humidity, and poor soil. If the seeds are left
on the plant, you may see goldfinches feed on them during the winter.
Butterflies and other birds are attracted to this plant also. Flower colors
vary, but the most common one is lilac. The petals lean downward
more than a daisy. Zones 3-9. In ideal conditions, they can reach five
feet high and two feet wide.

Coralbell (heuchera sp) (HEW-ker-ah)

Coralbells are native to the Midwest and are a popular groundcover. Some gardeners take the flower buds off to encourage growth outward. The flowers are greenish-white with a red tinge and appear in early summer. They tower over the plant on thin stems, occasionally three feet tall. In northern areas, plant them in full sun and cover them with mulch for the winter. Zones 3-9, Rutgers rating B.

Coralberry "Snowberry" (symphoricarpos albus) (sim-for-ee-KAR-poss AL-bus)

The Coralberry shrub, also known as Waxberry, is easily grown in average soil in full sun or part sun, with full sun yielding the best fruit production. It adapts to many soil conditions including poor ones. Prune as needed in late winter or early spring. Native to Eastern North America, it grows to a rounded shrub about six feet in any direction in Zones 3-7. Summer pink blooms precede pale green berries that lighten to white by early autumn. Birds don't especially like the berries, so they add interest to the winter landscape. Their tendency to spread by suckering makes them ideal for erosion control on rocky slopes, but be careful to keep them contained. Don't eat the berries! They're poisonous.

Coreopsis (coreopsis sp) (kor-ee-OP-sis)

Coreopsis, sometimes called Tickweed, is characterized by bright yellow flowers that bloom in the summer in Zones 3-9. The plants can grow to two feet tall but are usually less than a foot tall. They tolerate dry soil well but need full sun. Butterflies are a fan of this plant. The hairy texture of the leaves is a big turn-off to deer.

Corydalis (corydalis sp) (kor-ID-ah-liss)

Corydalis plants thrive in heavy shade and produce blue, purple, white, pink, or yellow flowers from early spring to frost. Wet
feet in wintertime can be fatal, however, so make sure your soil is
well-drained. It grows better in England than in America, because of
England's cooler temperatures. It reaches about a foot and a half high
and a foot and a half wide. It may self-seed. Zones 5-8, Rutgers rating
A.

Cosmos (cosmos sp) (KOZ-mose)

Cosmos is a plant native to the southern US and Mexico which grows well in average, well-drained soils in full sun in Zones 2-11. It is an annual, so plant the seeds outside just before the last spring frost date. Shelter plants from strong winds and plant them close together so they can use each other for support as they grow taller. Some can reach four feet tall.

Cotoneaster (cotoneaster) (kot-on-ee-ASS-ter)

Cotoneaster shrubs originated in Siberia and China, so you know they can handle Minnesota winters. Rated for Zones 4-7, they grow to ten feet high and just as wide. Seeds or cuttings spread them. Once established, they can withstand some drought conditions and can tolerate poor soil. Mulch the ground under the plant to discourage weeds from coming up within the plant, where they are hard to reach. Flowers are small and white with a pink tinge and are followed by small oval fruits. The redeeming quality of this plant is its impressive orange-red color in the fall. It is rabbit-resistant as well. It likes full sun but can do just as well in partial sun conditions. Rutgers rating B.

Cotoneaster Bearberry (cotoneaster dammeri) (kot-on-ee-ASS-ter DAM-mer-ee)

Cotoneaster Bearberry plants are a subspecies of Cotoneaster that are ground covers, only a foot high at the most. They spread easily and must be pruned. But if you often forget to water your plants, this is the one for you. Once established, it rarely needs watering. White flowers with purple anthers in spring/summer are followed by red berries in the fall. These berries persist throughout winter unless eaten by birds. Rutgers rating B, rabbit-resistant, full sun or partial sun, Zones 4-7.

Creeper, Trumpet (campsis radicans) (KAMP-sis RAD-ih-kanz)

Trumpet Creepers originate in the southeastern US but can grow in Zones 4-8. They like full sun but can grow in partial sun, but with fewer blooms. Once it is established, the main problem is how to stop it from spreading, so give it lots of room. Prune it in the spring, and it won't affect the flowering that summer. Make sure the structure you want it to climb is sturdy because these plants get heavy. Red, trumpet-like flowers show off all summer, and the seed pods in the fall can disperse this plant all over the place. Be careful when around the plant because some people get itchy after coming in contact with the leaves. It attracts hummingbirds.

Crocus (crocus) (KROH-kus)

Crocus blooms are often the first sign of spring and can be seen popping up through the snow just when you thought winter was going to last forever. Plant them in corners around the outside of the house where they will not be bothered. Warning: squirrels love digging up the newly planted bulbs (actually called corms) and they are quite adept at finding them. They originated in the Alpine areas of Europe and are rated for Zones 3-8. The blooms are generally white or purplish, and the leaves look like grass. About six weeks after blooming, they should be allowed to dry out a bit, which is why I recommend not putting them all over. Otherwise, you would be underwatering something else to avoid overwatering these during dormancy. Rutgers rating B. They rarely get above six inches high or wide but are a very welcome sight in March.

Crosomia (crosomia sp) (kro-SO-mee-uh)

Crosomia, also called Montbretia, calls out to all hummingbirds in the summer with its abundance of little red, orange, or yellow blossoms grouped along a stem. It requires full sun and thrives in Zones 6-10. It can grow up to eight feet tall and has a Rutgers rating of B. Rabbit resistant.

Crown Imperial (fritillaria imperialis 'lutea') (frit-il-AR-ee-uh im-peer-ee-AL-is LOO-tee-uh)

The Crown Imperial lives up to its name. The upward spiky leaves above the downward drooping yellow petals are quite impressive and do resemble a crown. The stalks are four feet high, adding to the wow factor. It blooms in spring/summer and requires full sun or at least partial sun. In northern areas, plant them in full sun. In southern areas, they can tolerate partial sun. Bulbs should be planted sideways to prevent water from collecting in the hollow of the bulb and causing bulb rot. The whole plant smells skunky, which repels deer, rabbits, and humans alike. They do well at the back of a garden where they can get tall and not offend our tender noses. Blooms from other varieties can come in purple, white, orange, and red.

Cucumber (cucumis sativus) (KOO-koo-mis sa-TEE-vus)

Everyone has had cucumbers at some point in their life. Little did we know that deer don't like it. Native to the East Indies, it can grow in Zones 2-11 and needs full sun. The yellow flowers show up in spring, followed by, you guessed it, cucumbers. Properly supported, it can climb up to 8 feet tall but prefers to crawl along the ground if no support is handy. Plant them after the last spring frost, then make sure their moisture needs are met throughout the season.

Cypress, Bald (taxodium distichum) (taks-OH-dee-um DIS-tik-um)

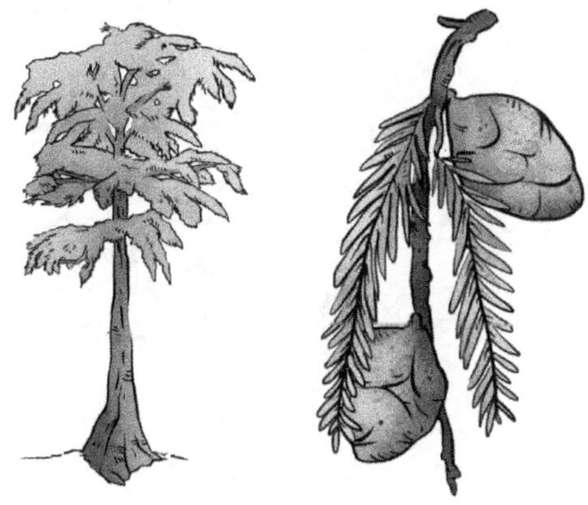

Bald Cypress looks like an Evergreen tree, but its leaves turn coppery-brown and fall off in the fall, thus earning the description Bald. It is found in Zones 4-10 and likes full or partial sun. It even tolerates moist soil and can be found along riverbanks. It is the state tree of Louisiana, and when found in the bayous, it develops knobby 'knees' where the roots take awkward angles. The deer dislike the needles because they tickle the nose. That's my theory, anyway.

Daffodil (narcissus) (nar-SIS-us)

Everyone likes to see the Daffodils rise in early spring, showing us that we have indeed survived another winter. When I lived in Lake Villa, Illinois, someone bequeathed a lot of money to plant daffodils, so you'd see them everywhere. The different varieties have slightly different colors but are basically a wide-petaled flower with a cup in the center, earning them the nickname Buttercup. In Zones 4-8, they thrive in full sun to partial shade and need well-drained soil. They can tolerate drought once established in their dormant season. Plant bulbs are four to ten inches apart and at least three inches deep. It may look sparse at first, but they self-multiply, and after a few years you'll have a sea of yellow. The 'actaea' variety is fairly tolerant of wet soils. They are poisonous to most deer, rabbits, and squirrels. They are often planted under trees, where they get enough sun in the spring before the tree's leaves obstruct the sun. Rutgers rating A.

Dahlia (dahlia sp) (DAH-lee-ah)

Dahlias are colorful to the point of being flamboyant and are synonymous with summer. They do best in southern locations but will grow in Zones 7-10. Dig up the tuber-like roots in the fall and store in damp (not wet) peat over the winter. Or plant them in pots and just drag them indoors. They are prone to pests so require a lot of maintenance. Some varieties grow up to three feet tall. Missouri Botanical Garden offered an ingenious solution if you don't like the height: dig a hole a foot deep, plant the tuber, then cover with six inches of soil. Gradually add soil as the plant grows. The different varieties come in every color except blue and bloom from summer to fall. They need full sun but will tolerate partial sun if the summers are scorching. They also attract butterflies.

Daisy, Shasta (leucanthemum x superbum) (lew-KAN-thee-num soo-PER-bum)

The Shasta Daisy is a man-made hybrid but the white petals with a yellow center are the image you see in your mind's eye when you hear the name daisy. In Zones 5-9, they will bloom all summer, growing up to three feet tall in full sun. They can grow in partial sun but will not have as many blooms. Deadhead spent flowers. Divide every two or three years. Wet soils in winter can be fatal, so make sure you have well-drained soil. They can tolerate dry soil. They are rabbit-resistant as well. Butterfly attractors.

Delphinium (delphinium sp) (del-FIN-ee-um)

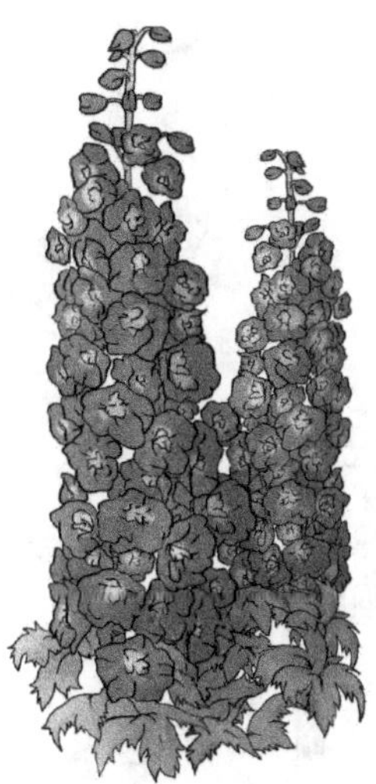

Delphiniums or Larkspurs are a common sight in vases or bridal bouquets. I had some myself. Their trailing stems of blue, purple, white, or yellow flowers offer a nice contrast to compact blooms of other species. They require some maintenance as they are susceptible to many pests, powdery mildew, and crown rot. Water them at the base to prevent wetting the blooms. They thrive in full sun and prefer cool summers but can be damaged by strong winds and rainstorms. Plant them near a wall, or be ready to stake them as they can reach three feet tall. Zones 3-7, Rutgers rating B, and rabbit-resistant. Butterfly and hummingbird attractors. Alkaline soil is best.

Deutzia (deutzia) (DOOT-zee-uh)

Deutzias are dense shrubs that can be used for an informal hedge. The shrub is covered in tiny white flowers in the spring for two weeks, and the fragrance repels deer but not humans. It is native to Japan but can be grown in Zones 5-8 with full sun or partial sun. It can grow to twenty feet high, but usually only five feet, and spreads to about five feet across. Rutgers rating B.

Devil's Walking Stick (aralia spinosa) (uh-RAY-lee-uh spy-NO-suh)

The Devil's Walking Stick, or sometimes called the Hercules Club, gets its name from the spiny thorns on the main trunk. It is native to the eastern US and thrives in Zones 4-9, growing to 15 feet tall in full sun or partial sun. The small white flowers arrive in the summer, giving way to black fruit and yellow to reddish-purple leaves in the fall. Some people get allergic reactions from touching the bark, so be careful pruning. And do prune, as it spreads rapidly. Bees love the flowers, but birds wait for the fruit to nibble on. Rutgers rating A. Other names are Angelica tree and Prickly Ash.

Dill (anethum graveolens) (ah-NEE-thum grav-ee-OH-lenz)

Dill is a common sight in vegetable gardens. The leaves are used to season soups, fish, vegetables, salads, sauces, breads, and herb butters. The seeds are more pungent and are used in pickles, sauerkraut, root vegetables, and teas. The flower heads are used in flower arrangements. An all-around useful plant, I'd say. They grow to three to five feet tall with long slender stems and blue-green leaves. Small yellow-green flowers appear in mid-summer, followed by the seeds. Leaves taste the best when harvested just after the flowers bloom. They do best in full sun and are prone to falling over in partial sun. Shelter them from strong winds as well, which will cause them to fall over. It can grow in Zones 2-11 but prefers cool summers. Rutgers rating B.

Dogwood, Flowering (cormus) (KOR-mus)

The Flowering Dogwood tree grows fast and spreads fast, so keep an eye on it if you want it confined. In Zones 3-7, it grows to about ten feet tall. Flowers are small and white, followed by white fruit tinged with blue-green, which birds love. Leaves turn bright yellow in full sun but only greenish-yellow in partial shade. Once established, it can tolerate dry soil as well as occasional standing water. Pruning is not required, but many gardeners prune it back about a quarter or even to eight inches off the ground every two to three years to stimulate better color. Rabbit-resistant.

Dusty Miller (jacobaea maritima) (jak-koh-BAY-ee-uh mah-RIT-ih-mah)

Dusty Millers, also known as Silver Ragwort, is winter hardy in Zones 7-10 but can be grown as an annual north of that area. It rarely flowers and only reaches a foot and a half tall and a foot wide. It prefers full sun or partial sun but can tolerate shade. Some gardeners take cuttings to plant the following spring, while others just buy new seedlings. The gray color and fuzzy feel of the leaves annoy the deer. Rutgers rating A.

Elder (sambucus) (sam-BYOO-kus)

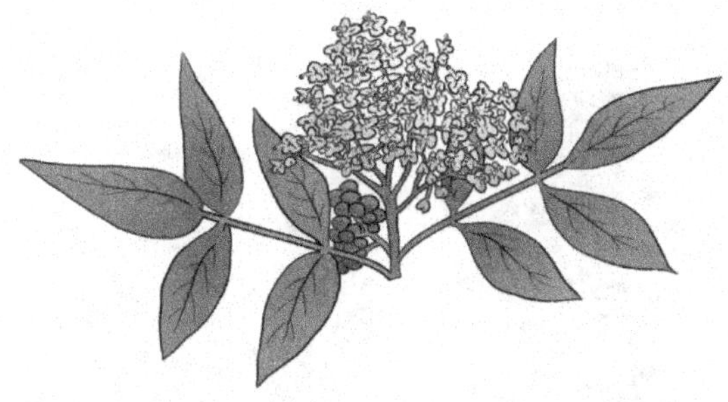

The Elder, sometimes called Elderberry, is a sprawling shrub that can tolerate wet soils, making it ideal for along rivers. In Zones 3-9, it prefers full sun but can tolerate partial sun. Heavy snow in the winter can damage branches so you may want to prune this shrub severely in the fall. It has the best yellow foliage in full sun. Tiny white lemon-scented flowers appear in early summer, attracting butterflies, giving way to black berries, which birds like and humans can make into elderberry jam. Rutgers rating B. Max height twelve feet and width ten feet. It spreads with suckers, so prune them away if you don't want it to grow out of bounds. Elderberry tea may help reduce a fever. Elder bark tea is a folk remedy for fighting colds and sore throats.

Elm (ulmus) (ULM-us)

The Elm tree was a common sight until Dutch Elm Disease ravaged them. Now some varieties are resistant to that blight. They prefer full sun in Zones 4-9 and have very insignificant green flowers in the spring. In the fall, the seed pods fly away on wings that resemble flying saucers. They commonly reach forty feet high and are fast-growing. Slippery Elm bark tea may relieve a sore throat. Some use it with mint for stomach pain. Traditional herbal medicine sources recommend it for an irritated digestive tract. It is also used to treat asthma. An all-around useful herb, I would say.

Fennel (foeniculum vulgare) (foe-NIK-yew-lum vul-GAR-ay)

Fennel has been used for a long time in the kitchen: the leaves in salads, potatoes, and fish, and the seeds as flavorings in bakery products and sausages. They are a favored plant for swallowtail butterfly larvae. They grow to five feet tall and contain aromatic feathery leaves in needle-like segments. Flowers, attractive to butterflies, bloom in mid to late summer and give way to aromatic seeds.

Fern, Christmas (polystichum acrostichoides) (pol-ISS-tih-kum ak-roe-stik-OY-deez)

Christmas Ferns are often found in forests but can be used on hillsides to prevent soil erosion. The ferns form clumps that grow in size but do not generally spread. They reach two feet high and two feet wide in Zones 3-9 and live in partial sun and full shade. Since they stay green through the winter, they are a winter interest plant for the garden. Rabbit-resistant. Rutgers rating A.

Fern,   Cinnamon   (osmundastrum   cinnamomeum)
(os-muhn-DAH-strum sin-uh-MOH-nee-um)

Cinnamon Ferns are native to the US and are in many forests. Their upright fronds turn brown early in the season, giving them their name. They grow mostly in boggy ground and along shady ledges and bluffs. Fiber from this plant is used in the potting of orchids. In Zones 3-9, they can reach three feet high and three feet wide. Rabbit-resistant. Rutgers rating A.

Fern, Holly (cyrtomium falcatum) (sir-TOE-mee-um fal-KAY-tum)

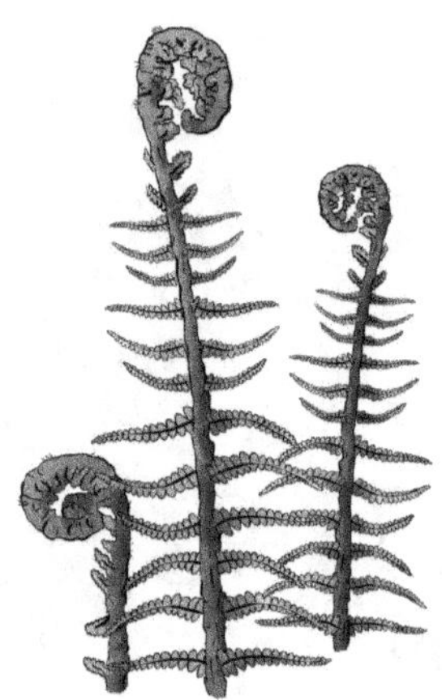

Holly Ferns, also called Japanese Holly Ferns, are found in Zones 6-10 and love partial sun and shade conditions. They need good drainage to survive or the roots will rot in the winter. Plant in sheltered locations. For areas north of Zone 6, they make great houseplants. Rabbit-resistant.

Fern, Sensitive (onoclea sensibilis) (on-oh-KLEE-uh sen-si-BIL-iss)

Sensitive Ferns are best used alongside streams and in wet woodland gardens. Allowing the soil to dry out will kill this plant, so be aware if you have it in a pot. It is sensitive to the first frost as well as drought. In Zones 4-8, it can reach four feet high and as wide. Partial sun or full shade is fine with this plant. Rabbit-resistant. Rutgers rating A.

Fir, Douglas (pseudotsuga menziesii) (SOO-doh SOO-guh menz-ESS-ee-eye)

The Douglas Fir is one of the largest trees in the world and is native to the Pacific Northwest. It can be grown in Zones 4-6, but I wouldn't recommend it in town as it grows up to eighty feet tall. If left to its own devices, it can grow to three hundred feet tall and doesn't mind higher elevations at all. It does not like drought or hot summers. It requires full sun. Deer don't like the prickly branches or their aroma when touched. Rutgers rating B.

Flag, Sweet (acorus sp) (AK-or-us)

Sweet Flag is a rush that actually likes to have its feet wet. Better it than me! If the soil is allowed to dry out, the tips of the leaves will turn brown. Settlers brought it over in the 1600s from Europe. It likes full sun or partial sun but will tolerate full shade if you don't expect too much from it. Use it in low-lying sections of your garden where water tends to stand. It is wide-ranging in America, growing in Zones 4-11. Rutgers rating A.

Flax, Blue (linum perenne) (LIN-um per-EN-ee)

Blue Flax is a perennial plant whose flowers bloom only for a day. Cut back the stems by half after blooming. They look best when planted all over a large area; the sky blue blooms cover everything, even though the individual flowers are short-timers. They can tolerate shallow, dry, and rocky soils. In clay soil, the roots tend to be shallow, causing winter fatalities. In Zones 5-8, they do best in full sun or partial sun and can reach two feet tall. The stems look delicate but are so strong that their fibers were used in Europe to make linen and rope. Today, commercial flax farms produce linseed oil from the seeds and linen fibers from the stems.

Flower, Balloon (platycodon) (plat-ee-KO-don)

Balloon Flowers are named in honor of the balloon-shaped buds which suddenly burst into bloom. Native to Asia, they thrive in Zones 3-9 in full sun or partial sun. The flowers can be blue, white or pink, and bloom in summer through fall. As usual, deadheading prolongs the blooming period. They reach a foot and a half tall and spread to about a foot wide. Avoid planting them in wet soils as they need good drainage. Also, avoid transplanting them as the roots are very delicate. New-season plant stems emerge late in the spring, so wait until you see the new stems to cut down the old ones. If they get too tall, they may flop over, so consider pruning them by half in May, before the flowers bloom in June to August, or stake them.

Flower, Blanket (gaillardia) (gay-LAR-dee-uh)

The Blanket Flower is native to the northwestern US but will do well in Zones 3-10. The origin of its name is controversial. Some say it refers to the yellow, orange, and red colors of the flowers being similar to the colors found in Native American blankets. Others say it is because the blooms will blanket the ground. It is happiest in full sun and will reach three feet high. The flowers bloom from spring to fall, attracting butterflies. The tiny berries that follow the blooms attract birds, especially Goldfinches. It prefers moist, well-drained soils but will tolerate drought conditions. It will not tolerate clay soils.

Flower, Helen's (helenium autumnale) (hel-EE-nee-um aw-tum-NAH-lee)

Helen's Flower, also known as sneezeweed, is native to the US and can be grown in Zones 3-8 in full sun. The dried flowers and leaves were used as snuff in Colonial days, explaining the odd name. It is also odd that a native American plant is named for Helen of Troy, but I'll let the historians figure that out. Cut back plants by half in early June to avoid them getting tall enough to require staking. Cut them back by half after flowering and divide them every three or four years. The flowers are yellow and similar to daisies.

Flower, Pincushion (scabiosa caucasica) (skab-ee-OH-suh kaw-KAS-ee-kuh)

Pincushion Flowers are found in Zones 5-9. The flowers have pin-like stamens in the center. In years past, the prickly leaves were believed to cure the irritation of scurvy, explaining the Latin name scabiosa, meaning itch. It can not tolerate wet soils, especially in winter. It likes full sun but can tolerate partial sun if the summers get too hot. It reaches a foot and a half in height and spread. The pink, blue, purple, or white flowers bloom from April until the first frost and attract butterflies. Rutgers rating B.

Foamflower (tiarella cordifolia) (tee-ar-EL-lah kor-dih-FOE-lee-ah)

The Foamflower is a native American, thriving in partial sun or full shade in Zones 3-9. It likes wet, well-drained soil in summer, but wet feet in winter are fatal. The leaves turn reddish-brown in the fall, and the number that fall off in winter depends on the severity of the winter. It forms a mound nine to twelve inches high and one to two feet wide. Taking off the flower stalks after blooming will make the mound look better. The stalks have a foamy texture, giving rise to the name. Flowers are white or pink. Rutgers rating B. Rabbit-resistant.

Forsythia, Northern Sun (forsythia x intermedia) (for-SITH-ee-a ex in-ter-MEE-dee-uh)

The Northern Sun Forsythia is often the first bloom in the spring, the yellow flowers reminding you that winter will not last forever. The flower buds are in by mid-July, so don't prune after that or you'll kill the flowers for next year. They will not always flower well in Zone 5, as the flower buds will die if the temperature hits five below zero. Since they can spread widely, pruning back to almost ground level every four to five years is recommended. This plant isn't picky when it comes to other conditions. It will grow in full sun to partial sun, although the flowers will be less showy in partial sun. It tolerates poor soils and even drought once established. Rated for Zones 5-8, it grows to about six feet high and just as wide. Rutgers rating B.

Fothergilla (fothergilla) (foth-er-GIL-la)

Fothergillas are shrubs native to the southeastern US but can live in Zones 4-8. It prefers acidic soil, as do Rhododendrons, so you can plant them nearby. Its white, fragrant spring flowers resemble bottle brushes, which is why deer dislike them. It slowly reaches six feet in height and the same in width. It thrives in full sun but can tolerate partial sun or even shade. Rutgers rating B. Leaves turn yellow, orange, and even reddish-purple in the fall.

Four O'Clock (mirabilis jalapa) (meer-AB-ill-iss jah-LAH-pah)

Four O-Clock, sometimes called Marvel of Peru, is only hardy in Zones 9-11, so bring the tuberous roots in before frost. It also does well as a container plant. It can be started from seed after the last frost. It likes full sun or partial sun and blooms beautifully in pink, rose, yellow, magenta, white and red from June to the first frost. Flowers open in the late afternoon (around four o'clock) and stay open until the following morning. It attracts hummingbirds, butterflies, and birds. All parts of this plant are poisonous when ingested. Rabbit-resistant as well.

Foxglove (digitalis purpurea) (dij-ih-TAL-iss per-per-EE-ah)

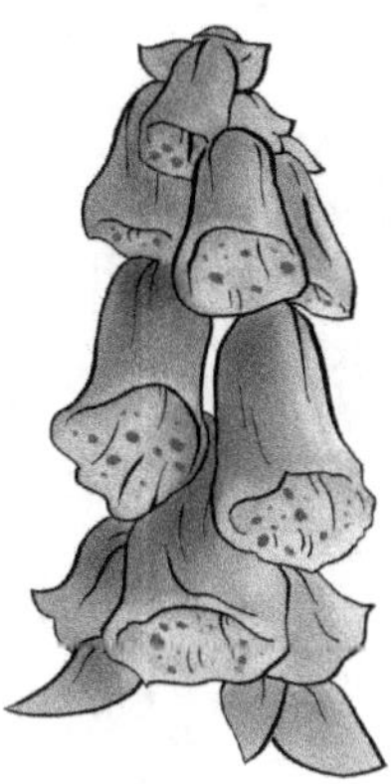

Foxglove is a source for the drug digitalis, used to treat heart conditions. Don't make tea from it, however, as the leaves are poisonous. The name comes from the shape of the flowers, which resemble fingertips cut off from a glove. The flowers are quite impressive: masses of them on tall spikes, like hollyhocks, who are cousins. The purple, pink or white blooms arrive in late summer, around when roses bloom. It prefers acidic, well-drained soil, and should not be left to dry out. It blooms best in full sun but can tolerate partial sun well. It can reach five feet tall, including the flower spikes, and is rated for Zones 3-8. Rutgers rating A. Rabbit-resistant.

Gentian (gentiana sp) (jen-shee-AN-uh)

Gentian, a native of Manitoba, can grow in Zones 3-7 in full sun to partial sun. The best flowering is in full sun, but hot summers and full sun can bleach the leaves. Flowers range in color from white or cream to greenish-white or blue and bloom from August to October. It is tolerant of slightly alkaline soils but must be well-drained, even to the point of being gravelly, as long as it is humus-rich. It usually reaches three feet tall and two feet wide. The name honors King Gentius of Illyria (reign 180-168 BCE), who discovered the medicinal uses of the root, from which tonic bitters are still made.

Geranium (geranium sp) (jer-AY-nee-um)

Geraniums love full sun. They can tolerate some drought but need that sunshine. There are two main kinds of geraniums. This one grows in Zones 5-8 to about eighteen inches high and twenty-four inches across. It attracts butterflies to its pink, blue, purple, or white flowers, but, frankly, smells bad. This is why both rabbits and deer avoid it. Some drought resistance. Rutgers rating B.

Geranium, Regal (pelargonium sp) (pel-ar-GO-nee-um)

Bring these Regal Geraniums in for the winter. They are only rated for Zones 10-11. But they are so profuse in their blooms that they are hard to resist. Put them in containers, dig up the roots of your favorites to store indoors, or just buy them each spring. They bloom in lavender, red, pink, and purple. They like the full sun as long as the summers aren't too hot. They need cool nights for the flowers to form. They are also called Martha Washington Geraniums.

Germander (teucrium chamaedrys) (TEW-kree-um kam-EE-driss)

Germander is an evergreen hedge that is native to Europe, northern Africa, and eastern Asia. It grows best in dry to medium moisture, well-drained soil in full sun. It can tolerate poor soil as long as the drainage is good. Plant them in a sheltered location and add some mulch for protection in our harsh winters. It is rated for Zones 5-11. Pinch after flowering to promote a more compact, bushy shape. It will reach only a foot in height and two feet wide. Its leaves are aromatic and oak-shaped and were previously used in medicinal applications. The small pink to purple (sometimes white) flowers arrive in late spring to early summer. Rabbit-resistant. Rutgers rating A.

Ginger, Wild (asarum canadense) (ah-SAR-um kan-ah-DEN-see)

Wild Ginger is native to the US and Canada and was used in colonial times as a ginger substitute, as the roots taste a bit like ginger. It loves shade, partial and full, and medium to wet soil, as long as it is well-drained. The spring flowers are hard to see as they are near the ground and often covered by foliage, but are a purplish-brown. Zones 3-8, Rutgers rating A.

Ginkgo (ginkgo biloba) (GING-ko bi-LOW-buh)

Ginkgo trees were a favorite of Frank Lloyd Wright in his landscaping designs, and I often drove past them in Oak Park, Illinois on my way to work. They turn yellow in the fall. Make sure you only plant male trees, as the female trees produce fruit that smells awful when they ripen and split. Ginkgos are considered the only surviving tree that was on Earth 150 million years ago. It will reach a hundred feet tall if left alone. It requires full sun and thrives in Zones 4-9. The spring blooms are green, so they are hard to spot. It is tolerant of salt, making it good along a road. They are also called Maidenhair trees. Tea from the leaves may be used as a remedy for all sorts of ailments as it is said to improve circulation.

Gladiolus (gladiolus sp) (glad-ee-OH-lus)

Gladiolus always reminds me of my grandmother's garden. She had a row of them in various colors, blue, purple, green, red, orange, white, pink, and yellow. They can grow up to six feet tall and can overwinter in Zones 5-10. My grandmother brought the bulbs into the cellar for the winter, as she was in Michigan's upper peninsula. They require full sun and have a Rutgers rating of B. If you're above Zone 7, you should bring your bulbs inside for the winter also. Try to protect them from strong winds.

Glory-of-the-Snow (chionodoxa luciliae) (kye-oh-no-DOKS-uh luh-SIL-ee-ay)

As you might suspect from the name, Glory of the Snow emerges in early spring when there is some snow left on the ground, and mixes well with other early bloomers such as Tulips, Daffodils, and Snowdrops. Plant bulbs about three inches deep and three inches apart in the fall and they will naturalize to form a carpet of blooms. You can plant them under deciduous trees, as they are already dormant when the tree's leaves appear. They are native to western Turkey and can be grown in Zones 3-8. Flowers can be blue, pink, or white.

Golddust (aucuba japonica) (AWK-yoo-bah juh-PON-ih-kuh)

Golddust, also called Spotted Laurel, is native to China's riverbanks and can be grown in Zones 6-10. It prefers partial sun or full shade, and can reach ten feet in height and six feet in spread. The white blooms arrive in spring, slightly larger on the male plant. Be sure you plant male and female plants together if you want berries. Protect it from wind, especially in northern Zones. If you are north of Zone 6, put it in a container and bring it in for the winter. It likes winter temperatures of 50-65 degrees, so don't put it in the den. You can grow it as a houseplant as well, and it will keep its leaves year-round. It is drought-resistant and has a Rutgers rating of B.

Goldenrod (solidago hybrids) (so-li-DAU-go)

Be careful with Goldenrods. They will take over the joint. Plant them in isolated areas where you don't mind their almost invasive capacity to spread. They have been declared invasive in China and many parts of Europe. They will grow in Zones 3-9 to about five feet high and five feet wide and will spread by creeping rhizomes and self-seeding. The yellow blooms arrive in summer and attract butterflies. They like full or partial sun and have a Rutgers rating of B. The leaves have sharply toothed edges, which may explain their deer resistance.

Grape (vitis coignetiae) (VEE-tiss koin-NAY-ee-ay)

This Ornamental Grape Vine is fast-growing, able to climb to 60 feet or fill a 1000 square foot trellis in a few years. It grows in partial sun, but prefers full sun and grows best in medium moisture with well-drained soil. Its green flowers arrive in summer. Zones 4-10. Prune back in the fall to avoid rampant growth. Rabbit-resistant.

Grass, Blue Fescue (FESS-cue) (festuca sp) (fes-TOO-kah)

Blue Fescue Grass is native to central and southern Europe and can be grown in Zones 4-8 in dry or medium moisture soil with full sun or partial sun. It reaches about a foot high and a foot and a half wide. It tends to die out in the middle so needs to be divided and replanted every two to three years. It is tolerant of drought and dry soils, but will not survive wet, poorly-drained soils. Foliage is semi-evergreen; in mild winters it may retain its blue-gray color, but will all turn brown in severe winters. Prune it back to three or four inches every spring anyway. The green with purplish tinge, rather insignificant flowers arrive in summer.

Grass, Blue Oat (helictotrichon sempervirens) (hel-ik-toe-TRY-kon sem-per-VEER-enz)

Blue Oat Grass is native to France and Italy and can be grown in Zones 4-8 in medium to dry soils with full sun. They will benefit from being cut back in the fall. The blue color is best in dry soils. This ornamental grass has bluish-brown flowers on spikes that rise above the grass in June, gradually becoming golden-brown in the fall. It reaches two feet tall and two feet wide, up to three feet high once the flowers arrive. Rutgers rating A is probably from the grass' porcupine-like structure.

Grass, Feather Reed (calamagrostis x acutiflora) (ka-la-mo-GROSS-tis ah-kew-tih-FLOW-rah)

Feather Reed Grass is a tall, erect grass that can serve as a narrow accent in your garden or a backdrop. Not only do the plants become three feet high, but the green, white or pink flowers also rise to five feet tall when they arrive in summer. It does best in medium to wet soils in full sun in Zones 4-9. It will grow in partial sun as well, but with fewer blooms and floppier foliage. Prune clumps to the ground in late winter. Rutgers rating A.

Grass,   Oriental   Fountain   (pennisetum   orientale)
(pen-nih-SEE-tum or-ee-en-TAL-ee)

Oriental Fountain Grass gets its name from its flowers. They rise
to three feet high and look like fountains of pink fluffiness. The plant
does best with medium moisture, well-drained soil, and full sun. It
can live in partial sun, but the flowers won't be as showy. Zones 5-11,
Rutgers rating A, possibly from its grayish-green leaves.

Grass, Purple Love (eragrostis spectabilis) (er-uh-GROS-tis speck-TAB-ih-liss)

Purple Love Grass performs best in sandy, dry soils in hot, humid locations. It tolerates drought and poor soils but needs full sun. Found naturally along roads and railroads, it forms a disorganized clump about ten inches tall. In August, the flowers form a purplish cloud above the leaves. Grows in Zones 5-9, Rutgers rating A.

Grass, Ravenna (saccharum ravennae) (SAR-har-um rah-VEN-nay)

Ravenna Grass can be used as a living screen as the bluish-green fronds reach five feet, and the white flower stalks reach eight to twelve feet tall. It can be grown in Zones 5-10 in full sun and is drought-tolerant once established. Rutgers rating A.

Hard Rush, Purple (juncus inflexus) (JUN-kus in-FLEK-sus)

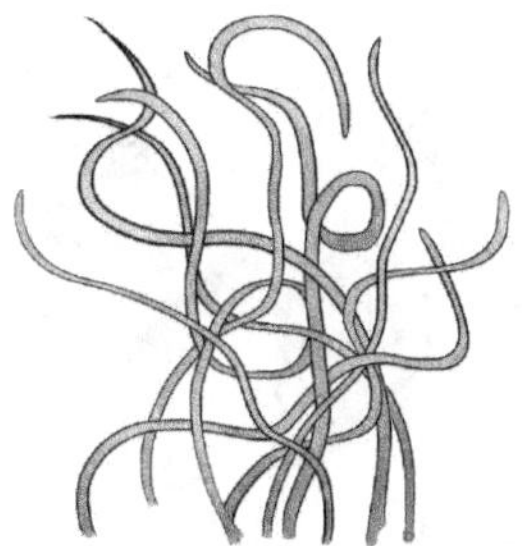

Purple Hard Rush plants technically have no leaves; they just have blue-green stems that taper to nothing at the ends. The flowers are hard to find as well, being brownish. The curved stems offer contrast in a rain garden or alongside a river, as it thrives in wet soil and even standing water. It only reaches eighteen inches high at best and spreads by rhizomes or by you dividing it every few years. It will tolerate light shade but does best in full sun. If any plants survive the winter, prune them back to a couple of inches in early spring anyway. Zones 4-10. Rutgers rating A.

Hawthorn, English (formerly crataegus laevigata, now crataegus rhytidophylla) (krah-TEE-gus ry-ti-do-FIL-uh)

We treasure English Hawthorn trees for their prolific white blooms in the spring, but deer don't like the thorns. Nobody does, which explains their widespread use in England in the 1800s as a hedge. They are also susceptible to many diseases and pests. In Zones 4-7 they can grow to twenty feet high with a spread just as wide, making them good shade trees. They do better in colder areas where the pests can't get such a stranglehold. Birds love the berries, which are also edible for humans. Butterflies love the blossoms. They do best in full sun and medium moisture soil. Rutgers rating B. Hawthorn extract is said to improve circulation and is considered by some to be good for throat problems.

Hazelnut (corylus americana) (KOR-ih-lus a-mer-ih-KAH-na)

The Hazelnut tree, also called a Filbert tree, is a shrub that can grow up to sixteen feet tall with a twelve-foot spread. A native American, it grows in Zones 3-9 in full sun or partial sun. There are separate male and female flowers on each plant, the male being more showy in yellowish-brown catkins, the female being smaller in red, inconspicuous catkins. Female flowers give way to nuts, which can be eaten or ground into flour but are usually left for the birds. The fall color depends on the variety. It is susceptible to Eastern Filbert Blight and is tolerant of clay soils. Rutgers rating B.

Heather (calluna sp) (kal-LOO-nuh)

Heather makes me think of Scotland with its moist, misty, cool weather. It dislikes the heat and humidity of the Midwest, so may not do well south of Zone 6. It is rated for Zones 4-8, however. It likes full sun to partial sun, and the white, blue, purple, or pink flowers arrive in summer, changing color along with the leaves in the fall. They have shallow roots, so be careful when you're digging in the area. Prune in spring before the new growth appears, especially if you have an older shrub that has become leggy and messy-looking. They reach eighteen inches tall and have a twenty-one-inch spread. It does not tolerate clay soil. Do not allow them to dry out. Rutgers rating A.

Heliotrope (heliotropium arborescens) (hee-lee-oh-TRO-pee-um ar-bor-RES-senz)

Heliotrope is an annual in the Midwest. It can not survive our winters, as seen by its rating of Zones 10-11. However, it is a popular annual and houseplant because of its prolific blue, purple or white flowers. It will reach a foot and a half high during the growing season. In Peru, where it originated, it can grow up to six feet tall, but they don't have to endure our winters. They prefer full sun but can tolerate partial sun with fewer blooms. The flowers are fragrant, which may repel the deer. Rutgers rating A. If you have a light spot in the house that is only around 50 degrees, you can overwinter these plants there.

Hens and Chicks (sempervivum sp) (sem-per-VEE-vum)

Hens and Chicks, also called House Leeks or Hens and Chickens, are very easy to grow in dry to medium soils in full sun, although they will tolerate some light shade. They like sandy or gravelly soils and tolerate poor soils as long as there is good drainage. I once killed mine because of overwatering, so learn from my mistake. After the hen flowers (in pink or white) and sets seed, it dies and the chicks fill in the gap. The leaves are edible and can be prepared like leeks. The plant is a succulent native to Europe, where they used to plant them on the roof, holding the slates in place, warding off fire, and providing emergency salad makings in the winter. Growing to half a foot to a foot tall, it makes a good ground cover. Zones 3-8.

Hibiscus, Blue River (hibiscus 'blue river') (hy-BIS-kus)

I thought Hibiscus plants could not be grown in the Midwest, so imagine my surprise upon seeing this hardy Blue River Hibiscus, which is rated for Zones 5-9. I know this leaves out some of the Midwest, but at least a few of us can enjoy the huge white flowers. It likes full sun and medium to wet soils. Do not let the soil dry out. Protect it from strong wind. Cut the plant back to three or four inches in late autumn. It will reach five feet tall and three feet wide in ideal conditions. The flowers only last a day, but there are so many of them, you don't really care. Deer don't like the serrated leaves, but butterflies love the flowers. New growth is slow to emerge in the spring. Don't be discouraged; it will grow rapidly once it starts. It will tolerate partial sun but does best in full sun.

Holly (ilex) (EYE-leks)

Holly reminds me of Christmas with its green leaves and red berries. If you want berries, make sure to plant both male and female plants. The serrated leaf edges irritate deer. The flowers arrive in spring, followed by berries in the fall. The berries remain throughout the winter if the birds don't gobble them up. Rated for Zones 3-10, it can reach twenty feet tall and likes full sun and partial sun. It appreciates the partial shade in hot summers and needs well-drained soil.

Holly, Sea (eryngium) (er-RIN-jee-um)

Sea Holly has leaves that look like holly leaves and flowers the color of the deep sea. Although you can get varieties with white or purple blooms, the usual ones remind me of thistles in that the petals come out of an oval pod. They are useful for cut or dried flower arrangements. Their height can reach three feet tall and spread to two feet wide. They may sprawl if they have less than full sun and should be left undisturbed once established and their taproots have gone deep into the soil. Sandy soil is preferred and it can tolerate poor soil as long as it is well-drained. Zones 4-10.

Honeysuckle (lonicera caerulea) (luh-NIS-er-a see-ROO-lee-uh)

Honeysuckle used to be my favorite fragrance as a teenager. This particular variety is different from other honeysuckles in that it produces edible blue fruit in the fall. Rated for Zones 2-7, it tolerates cold well and requires cool nights for best fruit quality. It prefers full sun but will tolerate partial sun, especially in southern regions. It reaches six feet tall and wide. Consistent moisture is essential in the early years, as it is drought-tolerant only when well-established. Plant two plants if you want fruit. Yellowish-white flowers arrive in the spring.

Hop Tree (ptelea trifoliata) (TEL-ee-uh try-foh-lee-AT-uh)

The Hop Tree is native to the eastern and midwestern US, and the seeds were used as Hop substitutes when making beer in colonial times. The unpleasant smell of its bark and leaves when bruised and flowers give it another nickname- Stinking Ash. It is easily grown in well-drained dry to medium soils in the shade and partial sun. It will tolerate full sun but does not prefer it. Rated for Zones 4-9, it is adaptable to a wide variety of growing conditions, and the smell keeps the deer away. The greenish-white flowers in the spring give way to seeds having a flat area all around, similar to Ash trees. It can grow to twenty feet high and to a spread of twenty feet as well.

Horehound   (marrubium   vulgare)   (ma-ROO-bee-um
vul-GAR-ay)

Horehound is a common ingredient in cough drops. It is related
to the mint family of plants. It has small white flowers that arrive in
the spring. Rated to Zones 3-9, it prefers full sun and good drainage,
although it will tolerate partial sun. It can become invasive if you don't
keep it in check by pruning in the fall. Deer and rabbits dislike the
smell, and deer also dislike the fuzzy and grayish color of the leaves,
earning a Rutgers rating of A. It is also drought-resistant.

Horseradish (armoracia rusticana) (ar-mor-AY-see-ah rus-tih-KAY-nah)

Horseradish is used in many sauces and condiments and can be grown in Zones 3-9 in medium soil. When you plant it, make sure you know its location, because any root bits left behind will form a plant the following year. It can crowd out other plants. Harvest the roots in the fall to use for cooking and save some to plant the following spring. It can grow to two and a half feet high and three feet wide and likes full sun. The little white flowers are easy to miss in the spring. Rutgers rating A.

Hosta, Hadspen Blue (hosta) (HOSS-tah)

Hadspen Blue Hostas have grayish-blue leaves, which deer don't appreciate. Be aware that some Hostas such as the variegated kind are delicious to deer and they will eat them down to the ground. Hostas will grow into a mound about eighteen inches high and twenty-four inches wide. Lavender-gray to off-white flowers arrive on stalks in the summer. Rated to Zones 3-9, they grow best in full shade, although some dappled light is tolerable. Keep the soil moisture consistent by watering the ground below the leaves. They should be divided every few years.

Hyacinth (hyacinthus) (hy-uh-SIN-thus)

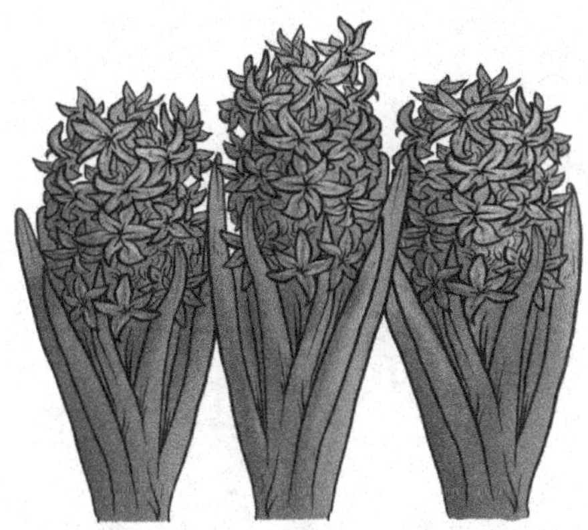

Hyacinths are famous for their flowers, which form spikes surrounded by blooms and are almost overpowering in their scent. The bulbs often decrease in their ability to bloom after the first year, so should be replaced every year or two. Bulbs can also be forced in pots for winter bloom. Wear gloves when handling the bulbs to avoid allergic reactions. The flowers come in a rainbow of colors: blue, purple, white, pink, red, and variegated or plain. Rated for Zones 4-9, they will grow in full or partial sun and medium well-drained soil. Plant in fall four to six inches apart. Plant about a dozen for the best effect. Keep the soil moist at first to encourage root growth, then taper off. Keep soil moist during bloom, then taper off as the plant goes dormant. The plants are small, only a foot tall, and half a foot wide. Rabbit-resistant and Rutgers rating B.

Hyacinth, Grape (muscari) (mus-KAR-ee)

Grape Hyacinths are similar to regular Hyacinths, but the bloom clusters are narrower. Rated for Zones 4-8, they reach only nine inches tall and six inches wide. Leaves come up in the fall to survive the winter, followed by spikes of flowers in the early spring in blue, purple, white, or yellow, adding a splash of color to an otherwise drab landscape. It likes full sun or partial sun and medium soil. It will tolerate clay soil. These bulbs can also be forced in pots for winter blooming. Rutgers rating B.

Hyssop (HISS-op) (hyssopus officinalis) (hiss-OP-us oh-fiss-ih-NAH-liss)

Hyssop has been around so long, it was mentioned in the Bible. It grows to about two feet high, spreads by any means, and thrives in medium to dry soils in full sun or partial sun. Its leaves are still used for seasoning soups, stews, sauces, salads, and meats. The oil from the leaves flavors Chartreuse liquor. Plants have naturalized along many US roads, and the blooms are attractive to bees and butterflies. Its aroma keeps the deer at bay. Grown in Zones 4-9, it can tolerate drought conditions once well established. The purple-blue flowers arrive in late summer, and you can also find varieties with white and pink blooms. Rutgers rating A.

Hyssop, Giant (agastache 'black adder') (ag-ah-STAK-ee)

Giant Hyssop resembles the regular Hyssop, but is larger, growing to three feet tall. The smoky-red-violet flowers grow from black buds, are quite showy, and bloom all summer. The gray-green leaves are quite fragrant, reminiscent of anise and licorice. Zoned for 6-9, it requires full sun but can tolerate partial sun. Plant them with southern exposure and leave the stems on for the winter if you're on the northern edge of that range.

Iris (iris) (EYE-ris)

Iris blooms remind me of Easter. They bloom in the late spring in Zones 3-10, like full sun but will tolerate partial sun, especially in the hot afternoon. The flowers are available in many colors, but the most common one is white. Water them consistently until after blooming ends. They do best in sandy ground with good drainage. When they get overcrowded, divide them and replant. Plant shallowly with a third of the plant above the soil and the roots spread out for support. They usually reach about three feet tall. You can plant these in the spring or the fall, but plants that have the winter to grow deep roots have a better chance of blooming next year.

Ironwood (ostrya virginiana) (OSS-tree-uh vir-jin-ee-AN-uh)

Ironwood trees, also known as Eastern Hop Hornbeam trees, are native to the Midwest down to Mexico, Zones 3-9. It will grow to twenty-five feet tall by twenty feet wide in full sun to part sun, with medium moisture soil. A low maintenance plant, it is popular for use as a street tree or shade tree. The flowers are easy to miss- reddish-brown male blooms and light green female blooms that appear on separate catkins on the same tree. The female catkins are followed by drooping clusters of sac-like seed-bearing pods which resemble hops. The leaves turn a dull yellow in the fall and often drop early.

Ivy, Boston (parthenocissus tricuspidata) (par-then-oh-SISS-us try-kusp-ih-DAH-tuh)

Boston Ivy is famous for adorning the walls of Ivy League Colleges (and Wrigley Field) and is infamous for spreading rapidly, even where you don't want it. Don't plant it near shingles or painted walls, as the little tendrils will get underneath and ruin them. I wouldn't recommend it around brick walls; I know it looks pretty, but the tendrils reach into the mortar between the bricks and loosen it. Native to Asia, it grows best in Zones 4-9. It will tolerate any soil, any amount of sun, and grow to fifty feet tall if permitted. The leaves hide the flowers and berries, but birds find those berries.

Jack-in-the-Pulpit (arisaema triphyllum) (air-uh-SEE-muh try-FIL-um)

Jack-in-the-Pulpit plants have flowers with greenish spathes with purplish flowers inside, making it look like someone is standing inside. You can plant them from seed, but they will then take five years to flower. Flowering plants produce only male flowers at first, but in later years will produce both. Female flowers will produce red berries in the fall. Roots are poisonous. In Zones 2-9, they like partial sun to full shade and medium to wet soils. They don't do well in clay soils. They can grow to two feet tall under ideal conditions. Rutgers rating A.

Jacob's Ladder (polemonium caeruleum) (pole-MONE-ee-um sir-EW-lee-um)

Jacob's Ladder gets its name from the leaves that can have up to twenty-seven leaflets on each leaf, making it look like a ladder. Able to grow in Zones 4-9, the plants prefer full shade but can tolerate partial sun. Too much sun will scorch the leaves. They grow to two feet tall, and the deep blue flowers arrive in the spring. They can easily self-seed, so deadhead the flowers if you want to keep them in check. They prefer cool summers and have a Rutgers rating of B.

Jasmine (JAZZ-minn) , Winter (jasminum nudiflorum) (jaz-MEE-num new-dih-FLOOR-um)

Winter Jasmine is a vine that forms a mound about four feet high with arching branches and trailing branches along the ground. It can grow fifteen feet long and performs best in sandy loams with regular moisture in full sun to partial sun. It can tolerate full shade, but won't flower as much. Native to China, it can grow in Zones 4-10. The yellow flowers arrive in the spring. Rutgers rating B.

Joe-Pye Weed (eutrochium) (ew-TROKE-ee-um)

Joe-Pye Weed grows in medium to wet soils and is seen at the edges of streams. It can grow into a clump seven feet tall and four feet wide. The flowers are dull pink and vanilla-scented, arriving in midsummer to the delight of butterflies. The seed pods last well into winter. Zone 3-10 rating. It requires full sun or partial sun, possibly requiring stem support if in partial sun. Prune back to the ground in late winter. The unusual flowers and seed pods make a valuable addition to cut flower arrangements.

Juniper, Chinese (juniperus chinensis) (jew-NIP-er-us chi-NEN-sis)

The Chinese Juniper is usually grown as a tree, reaching fifty feet high with a thirty-foot spread, but it can also be grown as a shrub. Native to China (you guessed that from the title), it is rated for Zones 4-9 and has a Rutgers rating of B. It needs full sun and well-drained soil and is not tolerant of clay or wet soils. Male plants produce Catkin-like pollen cones. Female plants produce seed-bearing cones that take two years to mature.

Juniper, Common (juniperus communis) (jew-NIP-er-us KOM-yoo-nis)

The Common Juniper is a true Northerner, rated for Zones 2-6. Depending on your latitude, it can be a low groundcover or a shrub reaching fifteen feet high by twelve feet wide. It grows best in full sun with medium moisture, well-drained soil, and has good drought tolerance once established. It can also do well in rocky or dry soil. Plant male and female plants together to get berries, which take two to three years to ripen and are used to flavor gin. They are tolerant of salt, so you can plant them along the road if you wish. According to tradition, Juniper berries are said to relieve symptoms of urinary tract infections.

Kerria, Japanese (kerria japonica) (KER-ee-a juh-PON-ih-kuh)

Japanese Kerria is sometimes called the Easter Rose because the profuse yellow blooms arrive around Easter and the flowers resemble roses. Rated for Zones 4-9, it prefers partial sun to shade. The flowers can fade if exposed to too much sun. This shrub can grow to five feet tall by eight feet wide. Prune back after flowering, as the flowers grow on last year's growth. It doesn't like heavy clay soils but is tolerant of both dry and wet soil.

Lady's Mantle (alchemilla mollis) (al-kem-ILL-uh MAW-liss)

Lady's Mantle is a shrub that self-seeds almost to the point of becoming invasive, so keep that in mind when purchasing. Deadhead blooms to avoid self-seeding and possibly encourage another bloom. It can grow in Zones 3-8 in medium soil from full sun to partial sun. The chartreuse flowers arrive in June and can be cut and dried for dried flower arrangements later. Rutgers rating B and is also rabbit-resistant. It usually forms a clump about a foot high, not counting the flowers which add another foot. The leaves are shallow-toothed and a little hairy, making them pretty after rain but unattractive to deer.

Lamb's Ears (stachys byzantina) (STAK-iss biz-an-TEE-nuh)

Lamb's Ears have silver-gray fuzzy leaves, which explains the name. They do have spiky flowers in the summer, but many gardeners chop those off because they like the groundcover look. They only grow to about six inches tall, eighteen if you count the flowers, and spread to about eighteen inches wide. They prefer full sun and are rated to Zones 4-8. They are tolerant of dry soils and shallow, rocky soils, and are rabbit-resistant. Be careful of hot, humid summers as they are prone to rot and leaf diseases. Make sure the soil is well-drained. Rutgers rating A.

Lantana (lantana sp) (lan-TAN-ah)

Lantana is only rated for Zones 8-11, but it grows so fast it makes a popular annual and container plant. It grows to four feet tall and three feet wide with blooms from July to frost. The blooms come in a variety of colors, with different colors often appearing on the same plant. It needs full sun and has a Rutgers rating of B.

Larch (larix) (LAR-iks)

The Larch tree needs a lot of room to grow, reaching a hundred feet
tall and thirty feet wide. It likes cool summers and cold winters and is
rated for Zone 2-6. Its needles make you think it's an evergreen, but
they turn yellow in the fall and drop. It prefers moist, gravelly loams
and will not tolerate dry soil or city pollution. Rutgers rating A.

Larkspur (consolida ambigua) (kon-SOL-ih-dah am-BIG-yew-ah)

Larkspur is easily grown from seed in loose, moderately rich, well-drained soils with consistent moisture and full sun. Plant seeds in the early spring from nine to twelve inches apart. Avoid wet soils. It grows to about three feet tall, and the showy flowers arrive in late spring and last through summer. The flowers are primarily blue, but white and pink are not unheard of. Leaves, flowers, and seeds are poisonous if ingested. Zones 2-11. Rutgers rating A.

Laurel, Drooping (leucothoe fontanesiana) (loo-KOH-thoh-ee fon-tay-nee-zee-AH-na)

The Drooping Laurel is an evergreen bush native to the eastern US from New York south along the Appalachians. It grows best in moist, acidic, organically rich, cool, well-drained soils in partial shade. It can be grown in full sun if you water it consistently. It does not tolerate drought or high winds. It can also be grown in full shade. Rated for Zones 5-8, mulch it well and plant it in a protected location. The white flowers appear in May, and eventually, the plant will reach three feet high by three feet wide.

Laurel, Mountain (kalmia) (KAL-mee-uh)

Mountain Laurel can be grown in Zones 4-9 in cool, moist, acidic, well-drained soil. Mulch to keep roots cool and retain moisture. It can tolerate a wide variety of sunlight levels but does best in partial sun, having some morning light and afternoon shade. The flowers are rose to white with purple markings and arrive in late spring in a spectacular display. It grows into a dense shrub about fifteen feet high, growing gnarly with age. The leaves are leathery and glossy, which explains the plant's deer-resistant and rabbit-resistant ratings.

Lavender   (lavandula   angustifolia)   (lah-VAN-dew-lah
an-gus-tih-FOE-lee-ah)

Lavender, also called English Lavender, is so named because it does well in England's climate, not to mention the color of the flower petals. It grows best in well-drained, slightly alkaline soil in full sun. It will not tolerate wet soil and can develop root rot, especially in the winter. To combat high summer humidity, consider using rock mulch instead of organic mulch. Rated for Zones 4-8 and Rutgers A, it is also rabbit-resistant. It commonly grows to three feet high by four feet wide and should be pruned regularly. Deadhead the flowers after blooming. The flowers and leaves are fragrant, and the butterflies love the blooms. The flower petal oils are extracted to use in fragrances and for culinary purposes.

Lavender-Cotton (santolina chamaecyparissus) (san-toe-LEE-nah kam-ah-sip-ar-ISS-us)

Lavender-Cotton, sometimes called Gray Santolina, is a small shrub with aromatic, evergreen, silver-gray foliage. It grows in a mound up to two feet high and three feet wide, with yellow flowers arriving in the summer and reaching six inches above the shrub. They like dry to medium soil and full sun, tolerating limey soil. They can get fungal diseases in hot humid summers that kill the branches in the center of the mound. They need regular moisture during the first year but can tolerate drought afterward. Rutgers rating A, Zones 6-9.

Lemon Balm (melissa officianalis) (mel-ISS-a oh-fiss-ih-NAH-liss)

Lemon Balm leaves smell like, you guessed it, lemon when bruised, and is often used to make tea, added to soups, sauces, vegetables, and salads, and when dried for sachets and potpourri. Historically the leaves were used for claiming teas, as a poultice for insect bites, and ingested for stomach aches. The tiny white flowers are hard to see, but honey bees love them. The plant is easily grown in dry to medium, well-drained soils in full sun to partial sun. Frequent pruning will help the plant keep its bushy shape. In Zones 3-7, the plant can grow to two feet tall and spread to three feet wide. Rutgers rating A.

Liguria (lig-YOO-ree-uh), Rocket (ligularia 'the rocket') (lig-yoo-LAR-ee-uh)

Rocket Liguria, also called the Leopard Plant, is a mounding shrub five feet high and four feet wide that produces yellow flowers on spikes up to six feet tall in the summer. It is best grown in rich, medium to wet soils in partial sun to full shade in Zones 4-9, in areas sheltered from the wind. Never let the soil dry out. Rutgers rating A.

Lilac, Common (syringa vulgaris) (si-RING-gah vul-GAIR-iss)

One of my neighbors growing up had a Lilac bush. I used to detour to walk past it when it was blooming and pause to absorb the aroma. Lilacs can be found in Zones 3-7 and can grow to sixteen feet high with a twelve foot spread. The May blooms arrive in large clumps, like Hyacinths, and hummingbirds and butterflies love them. It can survive partial sun with fewer blooms, but it performs best in full sun. Rutgers rating B and rabbit-resistant.

Lily, Calla (KAL-uh) (zantedeschia sp) (zan-to-DES-kee-uh)

Calla Lilies are not in the lily family but are related to Jack-in-the-Pulpits. They are rated as Zone 8-10, so bring them in before the frost and store them in a sunny spot in a container. They make attractive houseplants when overwintering. Nothing in comparison with their spectacular beauty in the summer, though. When the huge blooms come up in the summer, they steal the show, and are commercially used as cut flowers. The plant itself grows to about three feet tall and two feet wide and enjoys full sun or partial sun. In the spring, plant them three to four inches deep and twelve to eighteen inches apart. They don't mind getting their feet wet; they can even be planted in mud underneath a foot of water. Rutgers rating B.

Lily, Canna (canna sp) (KAN-uh)

Canna Lilies are another plant that needs to be dug up in the fall, but the impressive foliage and flower colors are worth it. A friend of mine planted bright red canna lilies in front of her house where they announced summer when they bloomed. These plants are rated for Zones 7-10, so right before the first frost, bring them in if they are in containers, or dig them up and put them in some peat moss for the winter, spraying them occasionally so they don't dry out. Prune the flower stems after blooming and cut the whole plant down to the ground before taking it inside. Plant them four to six inches deep and twelve to eighteen inches apart after the threat of frost has passed. They grow up to eight feet tall and five feet wide with large leaves. The flowers come in a variety of colors such as red, orange, cream, pink and bicolor. Divide them in the spring before replanting if desired, keeping in mind only one flower per plant.

Lily, Toad (tricyrtis) (try-SER-tis)

The Toad Lily should be planted where you can see it at close range, as the spotted flower petals may not be as beautiful when viewed from afar. Native to the Philippines and the Himalayas, it is rated for Zones 5-9. It does best in medium to wet soil and partial sun to shade. It is popular because of its ability to bloom in full shade. The flowers are white with dark purple spotting. Make the soil slightly acidic and do not allow the soil to dry out. It will spread gradually and would appreciate a light mulch for the winter. It can be planted in the spring or fall.

Lily, Turf (liriope spicata) (lir-RYE-oh-pee spi-KAH-tuh)

The Turf Lily, also called Creeping Liriope, is a ground cover that reaches eighteen inches in height and twelve inches in spread, flowering in tiny, lavender to white blooms in the summer. It is in the Asparagus family, can spread aggressively, and should be mowed in the spring. It can help stabilize a slope. It prefers moist, well-drained soil in full sun to partial sun. Rutgers rating B and rabbit-resistant. Once established, it is drought-resistant as well. Zones 4-10.

Lobelia (lobelia) (lo-BEE-lee-ah)

Lobelias are annuals in the Midwest and have two varieties. The trailing kind is great for hanging baskets where the flowering vines can cascade down below the basket. The upright kind is better for planting in the soil and can reach nine inches high and twelve inches across. Native to South Africa, they are rated for only Zones 10-11 for overwintering. Most people buy seedlings in the spring, as they are hard to grow from seed. The blooms cover the entire bush in late spring and are blue to violet with yellow or white throats. They do well in full sun and partial sun, but bloom more profusely in full sun. They would appreciate some fertilizer every two weeks during the blooming season and may need to be cut back if the summers get too hot. Good for butterfly gardens. Rutgers rating B.

Lousewort,   Common   (pedicularis   canadensis)
(pe-dik-yoo-LAIR-is kan-a-DEN-sis)

The Common Lousewort sounds like a bug you need an exterminator for, but it is really a plant, and is also known as Wood Betony. It obtained its name from an old housewife's tale of domestic animals becoming more susceptible to lice infestation after eating these plants. It grows in Zones 4-8 up to a foot and a half tall with a spread of about a foot. The yellow or purple-red flowers arrive in the spring. It doesn't take much trouble and will flourish in full sun or partial sun, and may spread slowly by self-seeding.

Lungwort (pulmonaria sp) (pull-mon-AR-ee-ah)

Lungwort earned its name from its spotted leaves resembling a diseased lung, and was believed to treat breathing problems. Zoned for 2-9, it needs some shade but prefers full shade. It can reach nine inches tall and twelve inches wide and spreads slowly by creeping roots. It prefers moist, humusy soils that are kept consistently moist. Do not let the soil dry out, especially in the summer. The blue, purple, red, white, or pink flowers show up in April and should be deadheaded after blooming. Rutgers rating A. Powdery mildew can be a problem if the soil is allowed to dry out.

Lupine (lupinus sp) (loo-PY-nus)

Lupine plants can be grown as perennials, rated for Zones 4-9, but they do not grow well after a few years. Newly developed hybrids do better, but I would still recommend starting it from a seedling every spring. The late spring blooms come in a variety of colors- white, blue, purple, red, pink, yellow, or bicolor, and the spikes of intense color are impressive. They can grow up to four feet tall under full sun with slightly acidic, organically rich well-drained soil. In southern parts of the Midwest, I would suggest a little afternoon shade. Rutgers rating B and rabbit-resistant.

Maple, Full Moon (acer japonicum o-isami) (AY-ser juh-PON-ih-kum oh ih-SAH-mee)

Maple trees are a little confusing when it comes to deer-resistance. Rutgers gives the species as a whole a B rating, but Missouri Botanical Garden doesn't list deer-resistance on any of the numerous Maple trees. The variety acer japonicum o-isami or Full Moon Maple is rabbit-resistant. Maple trees as a whole have yellow to red coloring in the fall, making them stand out from other trees and making them my favorite. The small flowers arrive in the spring, followed by "helicopter seeds," officially known as winged samaras, which take the seeds far and wide. They can grow in full sun or partial sun, and the different varieties range from an eight foot tall shrub to a fifty foot tall tree. They can be grown in Zones 3-9 and are fairly drought-resistant once established.

Marigold, French (tagetes patula) (ta-JEE-teez pah-TOOL-uh)

French Marigolds and African Marigolds (tagetes erecta) are both deer-resistant. They are rated for Zones 2-11, but buy seedlings and plant them each spring for best results. They grow to a foot high and nine inches wide, and their aromas keep the deer away. They require full sun for the best yellow, orange, red, or bicolor flowers. I've heard that they are rabbit-resistant as well, but I can't find any proof. Rutgers rating B.

Marigold, Marsh (caltha palustris) (KAL-tha pal-US-triss)

Marsh Marigolds are not related to marigolds at all but are in the buttercup family. They look like buttercups, not marigolds. These plants are a good choice for pond edges and don't mind wet soil. Rated for Zones 3-7, they will reach a foot and a half in any direction and like full sun or partial sun. A little afternoon shade is welcome in the southern Midwest. Flower buds can be cooked and pickled in vinegar to use as a caper replacement. Young leaves are edible when boiled, but don't try to eat any of this plant raw. Rutgers rating B. They are also called Cowslips.

Marigold, Pot (calendula officinalis) (kuh-LEND-yew-lah oh-fi-shi-NAH-lis)

Pot Marigolds are in a third family. Marigolds like to confuse people, I think. These are rated for Zones 2-11 but dislike hot summers so much they might not last the season. They can thrive in full sun and partial sun, blooming better in full sun, making the butterflies happy. Their aroma repels deer and rabbits. They can reach two feet tall and two feet around. The boiled leaves were used in Shakespearean England for soups, salads, and rice dishes even though they are bitter. Rutgers rating A. They are usually grown as annuals but can reseed if you don't deadhead the flowers after blooming.

Marjoram   (mar-JOAR-um)   origanum   'rosenkuppel')
(oh-RIG-an-um)

This variety of Marjoram is not usually used for culinary purposes, but other varieties are. This plant is grown for its aromatic leaves and as a ground cover. Prune it back before blooming to keep the bush tidy. It does best in gritty, sandy loams in full sun and has good heat and drought tolerance. Rated for Zones 5-8, it reaches a foot and a half around with purple-red flowers in late summer and fall. Rutgers rating A.

Milkweed, Swamp (asclepias incarnata) (ass-KLE-pee-us in-kar-NAH-tuh)

Swamp Milkweed is another source for Monarch butterflies, in addition to the upland variety of Milkweed. Native to the US, it is a good choice for low-lying areas as it is found naturally in swamps, river bottomlands, and wet meadows. It can grow to four feet tall and has mauve, pink or white flowers that bloom in late summer. It likes full sun and will grow in Zones 3-9. Rutgers rating B.

Mint (mentha sp) (MEN-thuh)

Mint plants are easy to grow in any soil other than wet soil. Rated for Zones 5-8, it grows to about two feet tall and two feet wide with purplish flowers that bloom in the summer. It likes full sun or partial sun, depending on how hot your summers get. The fresh fragrant leaves can be used as a garnish or additive to food and drinks. Dried leaves are used for teas, sachets, and potpourri. Rutgers rating B.

Mint, Mountain (pycnanthemum pilosum) (pik-MAN-thee-mum pil-OH-sum)

Mountain Mint is rated for Zones 4-8 and is native to America. It grows to three feet tall and three feet wide with pink, purple, or white summer flowers. It likes full sun and partial sun and dry to medium soil. The leaves are a bit hairy and are aromatic when bruised, making them doubly distasteful to deer. This plant grows and spreads vigorously, so cut the roots around the plant in the spring to keep it in check.

Monkshood (aconitum sp) (ah-kon-EYE-tum)

Monkshood is native to Asia and gets its name from the flowers that develop into a shape similar to a helmet or monk's hood. They're rated for Zones 3-8 but have trouble with hot summer nights above 70 deg F. Theoretically, the plants can be divided, but they are better left undisturbed once established. They reach three feet in height and almost that much in width. The blue, purple, white, pink, or yellow flowers bloom in late summer. They like full sun or partial sun, medium to wet soils, and have a Rutgers rating of A. Be warned: any part of this plant is poisonous, and even touching the plant will cause problems. Do not plant anywhere near edible gardens or near where children will be playing. Wear gloves when handling the plant. Rabbit-resistant.

Moonflower (datura sp) (duh-TOO-ruh)

Moonflowers, also called Pricklyburrs, are rated for only Zones 9-10, so are grown as annuals in the Midwest. The creamy trumpet-shaped, lavender to pink flowers bloom in the evening and only last until noon the following day. The flowers are fragrant and bloom in the summer, followed by prickly fruit. In full sun, the plants will reach three feet high and spread out to six feet across. They belong to the nightshade family, and all parts are toxic.

Morning Glory (ipomea sp) (eye-poe-MEE-ah)

Morning Glory can grow almost anywhere, and once it establishes itself, it is nearly impossible to get rid of it. It can climb ten feet in a single season, and those tendrils can latch onto almost anything. They look pretty on a fence or trellis but keep an eye on it. Better to plant it in a hanging basket where it can be contained. It took over my vegetable garden no matter how many vines I pulled out. It is considered invasive in some states, and I can see why. The purple flowers bloom in the morning and close in the afternoon, hence the name. Rated for Zones 2-11, It likes full sun and attracts butterflies and birds.

Moss, Irish (sagina subulata) (sa-JI-nuh sub-yoo-LAH-tuh)

Irish Moss is a groundcover that doesn't mind being stepped on now and then, making it invaluable around paths. It is rated for Zones 4-7, likes full sun or partial sun, and rarely reaches six inches high. The tiny white flowers arrive in the summer. It is drought-tolerant once established and has a slight fragrance, keeping the deer away.

Mullein (mull-EYEn) (verbascum sp) (ver-BASS-kum)

Mullein has a two-year lifespan. The first year, the gray-green hairy leaves appear. The second year, a hairy spike with yellow flowers blooms all summer, leading to seeds and the death of the plant. It can tolerate dry soils and has naturalized all over the US. Some southern states have declared it invasive, so reconsider planting it in your garden. It was brought over from Europe by early settlers for its reported medicinal uses. The leaves contain an insecticide and a blood thinner. Tea made from the flowers has a reportedly calming effect. It is easily grown in dry to medium soils with good drainage. It prefers dry, rocky soils and needs full sun. Rutgers rating B, Zones 3-8. It can reach seven feet high in ideal conditions and can produce 180,000 seeds in its second year.

Myrtle, Crape (lagerstroemia indica) (la-ger-STREEM-ee-a
IN-dih-kuh)

Crape Myrtle is a shrub native to Asia that grows in Zones 6-9 in
full sun. The red, pink, or white flowers show up in the summer. It can
reach twenty-five feet high with a spread of twenty feet in the southern
US, but only about ten feet in the Midwest. Plant in protected areas
and apply mulch in winter as they are prone to die back almost to the
ground, depending on the severity of the winter. Rutgers rating B.

Nannyberry (viburnum lentago) (vy-BUR-num lent-AH-go)

Nannyberry plants are multi-stemmed shrubs that can also be trained to be single-stemmed trees. They grow in Zones 2-8 in full sun to partial sun in average, well-drained soils. Prune directly after flowering because buds form in summer for the following year. White flowers appear in the spring, giving way to blue-black berries in the fall that persist through the winter if the birds don't eat them up. These berries are edible and can be eaten off the plant or made into jams and preserves. Nanny goats are reported to have eaten the berries more than billy goats, which somehow caused the name. Once established, it resists drought and heat. The plants can reach sixteen feet tall in ideal conditions.

Nasturtium   (nas-TUR-shum)   (tropaeolum   majus)
(tro-PEE-oh-lum MAY-jus)

Nasturtiums are a common cut flower and annual in the Midwest. Rated for Zones 2-11, they need shade in hot summer afternoons in the southern regions. They do better in the northern areas where the summer doesn't get quite as hot. They can be trailing vines or bushy shrubs and can reach ten feet in height. The red, orange, yellow, or cream flowers do well in poor to medium, well-drained, slightly acidic soil. The fragrant flowers attract butterflies and repel the deer. Rutgers rating B.

Oak (quercus) (KWER-kus)

The Oak Tree does not have any aromatic flowers to drive the deer away. It simply is better at resisting the damage that deer inflict by rubbing their antlers against the bark. Grown all over America in Zones 3-8, it grows best in rich, acidic soil in full sun. It can tolerate clay soils and dry soils. It slowly grows to eighty feet tall and even one hundred feet tall in the wild. Make sure it has plenty of room to spread out to about eighty feet wide. Of course, it grows slowly, making it less popular among many gardeners. If you plant one today in your twenties, your grandchildren will enjoy it at full size. It also tends to outcompete other trees for the sun and can stump the growth of other trees by denying them light. The acidity of the soil around an Oak tree can damage other plants also.

Oats, Northern Sea (chasmanthium latifolium) (chas-MAN-thee-um lat-ih-FOH-lee-um)

Northern Sea Oats, also known as Indian Woodoats, is an ornamental grass native to the eastern US and rated for Zones 3-8. It ranges in height from two to five feet, with the spread half of the height. It prefers medium to wet soil and full sun to partial sun. It is more shade tolerant than many of the other ornamental grasses. Prune back to the ground in early spring. Dried, it makes an interesting contrast to dried flower arrangements, the seed pods turning coppery brown in the fall and drooping over a bit. Rutgers rating A.

Orange, Mock (philadelphus) (fil-uh-DEL-fuss)

Mock Orange shrubs are named because the late spring flowers reminded someone of Orange blossoms. Rated for Zones 3-8, it can not tolerate wet soil but does best in moist, well-drained soil and full sun or partial sun. Prune directly after the flowers fade, as next year's flowers grow on this year's growth. It may be pruned to the ground if it becomes scraggly. Usually grows to about four feet high and as wide.

Oregano (ore-REG-a-no), Herrenhausen (origanum vulgare) (oh-RIG-an-um vul-GAR-ay)

Oregano plants can't seem to do both things well: if they taste good, they don't look that great, and vice versa. Many varieties are available depending on what characteristics you want. The fresh and dried leaves are used in numerous Italian dishes. They can be grown in Zones 4-8 and prefer full sun and dry to medium moisture soils. Once established, they are drought-tolerant. The aroma of the leaves keeps the deer away. I don't think deer like Italian food anyway. Obtain cuttings from a plant that has proven superior taste. Rutgers rating A.

Pachysandra   (pachysandra   terminalis)   (pak-ih-SAN-druh term-in-AL-iss)

Japanese Pachysandra, sometimes just called Pachysandra, is a little thing, only reaching a foot high and a foot and a half wide. It likes partial sun to full sun; too much sun will bleach the leaves. It will do w ell under trees. Plant them six inches apart as they will propagate by rhizomes to become a carpet. You may need to thin them from time to time to keep the air circulating. Avoid watering the leaves. I know they're short but try watering the soil under the plants. Keep the moisture of the soil to medium. Rated for Zones 4-9. Rutgers rating A. Rabbit-resistant. The white spring flowers are tiny but quite pretty when viewed up close.

Pansy (viola sp) (vy-OH-lah)

Pansies were my mom's favorite flower. They can be planted as biennials, but it's easier just to buy the seedlings in the spring. In Zones 3-11, they can be found in a rainbow of colors around springtime. They never get over a foot tall and sometimes reach over a foot wide and require full sun or partial sun. The flowers are fragrant, which is why the deer avoid them and the butterflies adore them.

Parsley   (petroselinum   crispum)   (pet-ro-seh-LEE-num KRIS-pum)

Parsley is well known at the dinner table. It is used as a garnish on many things and the fresh or dried leaves are used for flavoring any number of dishes. Rated for Zones 2-11, it will grow biennially, but the flavor in the second year is inferior while the plant is flowering. Best to plant it as an annual every spring. It can tolerate partial sun but does best in full sun with medium moisture soils. Three main varieties of Parsley are Curly-Leaved, which is the most popular; Flat-Leaved or Italian, which has the strongest flavor; and Hamburg, which has a turnip-like root that is boiled and eaten as a vegetable. Rutgers rating B.

PawPaw (asimina triloba) (a-SEE-mee-nuh try-LO-buh)

PawPaw plants are small trees or large shrubs, depending on who you talk to, reaching thirty feet in height and width. They prefer full sun or partial sun and medium to wet soil and are found in Zones 5-9. The fragrant purple flowers arrive in late spring, followed by fruit, which is edible and used in ice cream and pie. Some people don't like them as they can upset their stomachs, but most people in the south look forward to eating them if they beat the wildlife (raccoons, squirrels, and opossums) to them. Plant two of them to get fruit. They spread by root suckers to form hedges and thickets. Rutgers rating A.

Pennyroyal (mentha pulegium) (MEN-thuh pul-ee-GEE-um)

Pennyroyal, sometimes called Fleabane for its insect repellent properties, is in the mint family, so deer don't like its smell. It can spread aggressively and has escaped gardens all over the US. Rated for Zones 6-9, it likes full sun or partial sun and moist, well-drained soil. It barely reaches a foot in height. The flowers are blue or purple and arrive in late summer or fall. It makes a nice addition to a cut flower arrangement and has been used as a herb for hundreds of years.

Penstemon (penstemon sp) (PEN-steh-mon)

Penstemon, sometimes called Beardtongue because its flower stamens have tufts of hairs, is native to the US, and can be grown in Zones
3-8. It can not tolerate wet or poorly drained soil and does best in dry
to medium soil and full sun. Different varieties are available that let
you choose what flower color you want, and hummingbirds like them
no matter what the color. Once established, it can tolerate drought and
clay soil. These plants can reach five feet in height and two feet wide.
The flowers are a welcome addition to the arrangement on the dining
room table.

Peony (paeonia sp) (pay-OH-nee-ah)

Peonies are famous for their large, beautiful spring flowers in red, orange, white, pink, and yellow. Even when not in bloom, these plants have dark green, leathery leaves that deer don't like, and they don't appreciate the fragrance of the blooms either. In Zones 3-8, they can grow to three feet in height in full sun. The tall stems may need staking once the flowers arrive, as they are a bit top-heavy. Rutgers rating A.

Pepper, Habanero (capsicum 'Chinese Roulette') (KAP-si-kum)

Habanero Peppers of the 'Chinese Roulette' variety are supposed not to be as hot as most Habanero Peppers, but I wouldn't touch them with a ten-foot pole. My stomach does not like hot peppers. They originated in Peru 8000 years ago, and Columbus brought them to Europe from the Caribbean. They are rated for Zones 2-11, but in the Midwest they are annuals, as they are killed by frost. You can grow them in containers and simply bring them in for the winter. They are members of the nightshade family and should not be planted in the same place a crop of tomatoes, peppers, or eggplants grew last year, as some diseases remain in the soil. They demand warm weather and full sun, and under ideal conditions can reach three feet high and two feet wide. The purple, white, or yellow flowers arrive in the spring. Deer share my dislike for these little guys.

Petunia (petunia sp) (peh-TOON-yah)

Petunias are second only to Impatiens in spring flower seedling sales. They come in three main varieties: Grandiflora, with blooms four inches across; Multiflora, with smaller blooms but more of them; and Cascading hybrids, used in hanging baskets. As they are rated for Zones 10-11, they are only annuals and don't try to grow next year's batch from seed. The hybrids do not seed true. The blooms come in any color except brown and black, arrive in May, and last until the first frost. They need full sun or partial sun and grow to a foot high with a spread of three feet. Great attractor for birds, hummingbirds, and butterflies.

Petunia, Wild (ruellia sp) (roo-EL-lee-ah)

Wild Petunias can be found in dryish soils in the Midwest such as open woods, prairies, and fields. It can reach two feet in any direction and has lavender-blue flowers from May to October. The Hawkeye Butterfly caterpillar feeds on this plant. It requires full sun or partial sun and dry to medium soil. The leaves are hairy, explaining the deer's dislike. Zones 4-8.

Phlox (phlox drummondii) (floks drum-AWN-dee-eye)

Phlox are great annual groundcovers with profuse blooms that last from May to July, longer in cooler areas. Native to Texas, they wilt during summer heat but revive in the fall. Buy seedlings and plant after the last frost or start from seeds 6-8 weeks before planting. It will grow in Zones 2-11 and prefers full sun or partial sun with medium soil moisture. The red, blue, white, or pink flowers are fragrant, repelling deer and attracting butterflies and hummingbirds.

Pine, Scotch (pinus sylvestris) (PY-nus sil-VESS-triss)

Scotch Pines are the only Pine trees native to Great Britain and are rated for Zones 2-9. They grow to sixty feet tall commonly and can reach one hundred and fifty feet in the wild. They need full sun and like acidic, well-drained soil. They are a Christmas tree favorite. Once established, they can tolerate poor soils, even clay or sandy soils, as long as the drainage is good. They are distinctive in the following ways: twisted, blue-green needles up to three inches long in bundles of two; gray to light brown cones up to three inches long; and scaly, orange-red bark near the top but darker reddish-brown near the base. They prefer cool summers. Rutgers rating B.

Pinks (dianthus sp) (dy-ANN-thus)

Pinks, commonly called Dianthus, Carnations, or Sweet Williams, are native to eastern Siberia and thrive in gritty, medium moisture soils in full sun for Zones 3-10. They only reach a foot tall usually but can get to three feet tall if sheltered from the wind. The flowers are of various colors, depending on the variety, and will attract butterflies. Flower colors range from purple and deep red to white and everything in between. Many varieties exist, some with double blooms. They can tolerate partial sun but will bloom less. They do best as biennials but are usually started from seedlings in the spring. If you're lucky, you can plant in the summer for blooms the following year, but don't count on it, especially with hybrids.

Plant, Creeping Shrubby Ice (ruschia pulvinaris) (ROOS-kee-uh pool-vin-AR-is)

The Creeping Shrubby Ice Plant is native to South Africa and can grow in Zones 6-10 in full sun and dry to medium soils. It can even tolerate rocky soils as long as the drainage is good. It only gets to about four inches high but can eventually cover a square foot of land. The pink or magenta-purple blooms last from April to June and blanket the entire plant, making it popular for butterflies. Rabbit-resistant.

Plant, Gas (dictamnus alba) (dik-TAM-nus AL-ba)

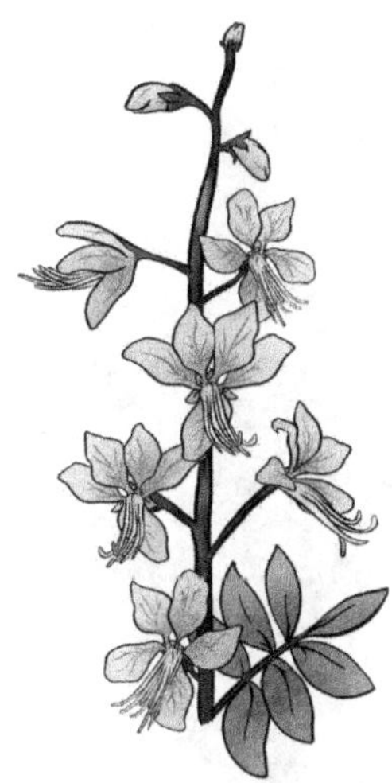

The Gas Plant, commonly called Dittany, earned its rather em-barrassing name by a flammable oil emitted by old flowers and seed pods, which can be ignited on still summer evenings. The leaf oil can cause allergic reactions on the skin but emits a lemony fragrance when crushed. It grows to four feet tall with fragrant white or pink flowers in late summer. Rated to Zones 3-8, it likes rich, humusy, moist soils but not soggy. Prefers full sun but can tolerate light shade and does best in northern areas where the nights are cool. It can be planted from seed but takes three to four years to establish and flower. Because it is so slow to establish, it can become a long-lived low-maintenance plant, tolerating drought once established. It is difficult to divide and best left undisturbed. Rutgers rating B.

Plant, Obedient (physostegia virginiana) (fy-so-STEE-jhah ver-jin-ee-AY-nah)

The Obedient Plant earns its name by the individual flowers staying in the direction they are pushed. Native to the eastern US, it spreads rapidly by rhizomes and self-seeding. The flowers are on spikes like snapdragons and range from white to pink to lilac, blooming from June to September. Rated for Zone 3-9, it requires full sun and moist, acidic, well-drained soils. Stems tend to flop in rich soils, too much shade, or hot summer temperatures and may require staking. They grow to four feet tall and three feet wide. Hummingbirds love them. Plant them in areas where they can't become invasive. Rutgers rating B.

Poker, Red Hot (kniphofia tritoma) (nip-HOFF-ee-uh tri-TOE-mah)

Red Hot Pokers, also known as Torch Lilies, are best grown in humus-rich, well-drained soils in full sun. It is tolerant of dry soil and does well in sandy soil. Wet, poorly-drained soil, especially in winter, will cause root rot. Plant in areas protected from wind, and in partial shade for southern areas of the Midwest. This plant is rated for Zones 5-8 and will grow to two feet tall by one and a half feet wide. The flowers are the distinctive part of this plant, blooming from bottom to top of the spikes and having tubular petals which droop down. There are many varieties of bloom color these days. Rabbit-resistant and Rutgers rating B.

Poppy, California (eschscholzia californica) (ash-SHOLZ-ee-ah
kal-ih-FOR-nih-kah)

The California Poppy is an annual easily grown in sandy, poor to
average, well-drained soils in full sun. It can be a perennial in southern
climates, but it may not survive our midwestern winters (even though
it is rated for Zones 4-10). It rises to a foot and a half high and just as
wide, with the orange bloom arriving in summer. It is the state flower
of California.

Poppy, Oriental (papaver orientale) (puh-PAY-ver or-ee-en-TAY-lee)

Oriental Poppies have showy, orange-red petals with purple centers, up to four inches wide, which arrive in late spring. The problem with poppies is that the leaves come up in the spring, then die out once the flowers appear, leaving a hole in the garden. This plant tries to self-seed, but the resulting plants do not come true, so remove stems after the blooms. Propagation by root cuttings is relatively easy, but plants should otherwise be left alone. It needs winter dormancy and is rated for Zones 3-7. It will grow to a foot and a half tall and just as wide. The leaves are thistle-like and grayish-green, explaining its deer repellent attribute.

Poppy, Plume (macleaya cordata) (ma-KLAY-uh kor-DAY-tuh)

The Plume Poppy is not exactly a poppy but it does have pretty white flowers in August. It grows from full sun to partial sun, depending on how hot that summer sun gets. Under ideal conditions, it can reach eight feet tall and four feet across. It spreads rather aggressively, so keep an eye on it. Rated for Zones 3-8, it is native to southeast Asia. It prefers sandy, well-drained loams. Rutgers rating B.

Primrose (primula sp) (PRIM-yew-luh)

Primroses only reach six inches high and spread by rhizomes, or you can divide them after the blooms are spent. The red flowers with yellow centers arrive in April, attracting butterflies. It prefers partial sun to full shade and moist, well-drained soil. Don't let the soil dry out. It is rated for Zones 2-8, and in northern areas can tolerate full sun.

Primrose, Evening (oenothera sp) (ee–no-THEE-ruh)

The Evening Primrose opens its flowers at dusk and closes them when the morning sun hits. The lemony fragrance the blooms emit attracts night-flying moths and bees in the early morning hours. In the first year, this plant produces no flowers. The second year, it dies after the lemon yellow flowers fade. Don't worry; it self-seeds, so there are more coming, although they might be somewhat leggy. The seed oil has been used for medicine, and Native Americans consumed the entire plant. It can reach five feet tall and three feet wide and is rated for Zones 4-9. It prefers average soils in full sun but can tolerate partial sun if the summers are hot. Rutgers rating B.

Queen of the Prairie (filipendula rubra) (fil-il-PEN-dyoo-luh ROO-bruh)

Queen of the Prairie plants can be spectacular when massed at the back of a garden. The pale pink summer flowers are quite beautiful and reminiscent of astilbe. It grows quite large, reaching eight feet tall and four feet wide, and is rated for Zones 3-8. It prefers full sun to partial sun and medium to wet well-drained soil. It can scorch in the sun if the soil is allowed to dry out. It is also called Meadowsweet.

Quinine (KWY-nine) , Wild (parthenium integrifolium)
(par-THEN-ee-um in-tuh-gree-FOE-lee-um)

Wild Quinine, also called American Feverfew, is a perennial native
to the eastern and midwestern US. Rated to Zones 4-8, it grows into a
clump four feet high by two feet wide, with the small clumps of wooly
white flowers arriving in late spring and lasting until late summer. It
is easily grown in medium to dry soil with full sun. The leaves are
aromatic and granular in texture, explaining its deer resistance.

Redbud, Eastern (cercis canadensis) (SER-sis ka-na-DEN-sis)

The Eastern Redbud tree is native to Eastern and Central North America and is the state tree of Oklahoma. It ranges from Canada to Texas in Zones 4-8 where it prefers full sun, although welcomes some afternoon shade in the South. The multi-trunk style makes it look more like a shrub than a tree. The tree doesn't like to be transplanted, so pick your site carefully. The rose-purple flowers arrive in April, on bare branches followed by seed pods that can remain on the tree all winter. The leaves can be blue-green or dark green, which may explain the deer's dislike. Butterflies love them. Under ideal conditions it can reach twenty feet high and a little wider than it is tall.

Redwood,   Dawn   (metasequoia   glyptostroboides)
(met-uh-see-KWOY-uh glip-toh-stroh-BOY-deez)

Dawn Redwood trees are deciduous, coniferous, and can grow up
to a hundred feet tall. The fossil record shows that they existed fifty
million years ago, but it wasn't until 1941 that any live trees were
discovered in China. As the tree grows, the trunk develops elabo-
rate fluting, which deepens into fissures as the tree ages. The foliage
is fern-like, feathery, and soft to the touch. Best grown in humusy,
medium to wet, well-drained soil in full sun, it requires a lot of room
to grow. Zones 4-8, Rutgers rating B.

Rhododendron (rhododendron) (roh-do-DEN-dron)

The Rhododendron genus includes about 900 species of both Rhododendrons and Azaleas, both evergreen and deciduous. They originate in the northern hemisphere and are grown for their showy white, pink, red, or purple spring flowers and, if evergreen, their winter foliage. True Rhododendrons have ten stamens in a flower, and Azaleas have only five. Most are rated for Zones 3-9 and grow to be about six feet tall and wide. They require full sun to partial sun and medium moisture, well-drained soil. Plant in an area protected from high winds and far from trees in the Walnut family (Walnuts, Butternuts, Pecans, and Hickories). Shallow root systems will benefit from mulching and require pH from 5.0 to 5.5 to thrive. Do not cultivate near roots and do not let them dry out. These plants are susceptible to many insect and disease problems. Rabbit-resistant. Rhododendron tea may be taken to allieve arthritic pain according to herbal medicine lore.

Rhubarb (rheum hybrids) (REE-um)

Rhubarb plants are a staple in any vegetable garden in Zones 3-8. It grows to three feet tall and four feet wide in full sun to partial sun and well-drained, slightly acidic soils. Best grown from root divisions (sections of root with one or more buds or eyes), which should be planted in early spring. Do not harvest stalks until the second year. Divide roots every four years or so. Tiny white flowers arrive at any time from May to late summer. The large, heart-shaped leaves are attractive but poisonous. The reddish-green stalks are edible and used in sauces, jams, and pies. Remove the leaves before cooking the stalks. Crown rot may occur in poorly-drained soils, and the plant does not like clay soils. Rabbit-resistant and Rutgers rating B.

Rock-Cress   (aubrieta   deltoidea)   (aw-bree-EH-tuh del-TOY-dee-uh)

As the name implies, Rock-Cress likes rocky soil and does well in rock gardens or even under spring-blooming bulbs. Perennial in Zones 4-8, it requires full sun for those purple, white, or pink blooms to look their best. This ground cover only reaches six inches high but spreads out to form a mat. Rutgers rating A.

Rose, Christmas or Lenten (helleborus nigra) (hel-LEB-or-us NY-grah)

The Christmas Rose has black roots, explaining the last part of the Latin name. It blooms around Christmastime, later in the winter farther north or if there has been a severe winter. Plant them in a sheltered location where you can see them and enjoy the red, white, pink, or green flowers when nothing else is blooming. Rated for Zones 3-8, they only grow to a height of one foot with a spread of a foot and a half. They like partial sun and shade, so can be planted along a wall, in a window box, or even under a deciduous tree. If ingested, the entire plant is <u>toxic</u> to humans, and maybe deer don't want to chance it either. The plants should be left undisturbed and will take a few years after planting to produce those beautiful flowers. Rutgers rating A. They propagate slowly through self-seeding.

Rose, Climbing (rosa sp) (ROH-za)

Climbing Roses have long canes, enabling them to hang onto any nearby support. They can reach twenty feet in a year. Rated for Zones 4-11, their blooms can be white, pink, red, orange, blue, or yellow. These plants require full sun and will develop more blooms if you train them to reach horizontally. Some varieties offer several blooms on a stem; other varieties have just one bloom per stem. Some varieties will bloom continuously, and other varieties will bloom just once in the summer.

Rose of Sharon (hibiscus syriacus) (hi-BIS-kus seer-ee-AK-us)

The Rose of Sharon shrub grows to twelve feet high by ten feet wide with abundant white to pink flowers from June to October in Zones 5-8. Native to China, it needs full sun to partial sun and medium moisture, well-drained soil. It can tolerate poor soil and some drought once established. Easily propagated from stem cuttings or seeds, but seeds may not have the same flower color as the parent. It can self-seed rather aggressively under optimum growing conditions, so keep an eye on it. Rutgers rating B.

Rosemary   (rosmarinus   officinalis)   (ross-mah-RYE-nus oh-fi-shi-NAH-lis)

Rosemary is only winter-hardy in Zones 7-10, so plant it in a container like a clay pot. During the winter, let the soil dry between waterings to prevent root rot and keep the air circulating, or it will develop powdery mildew. Provide six hours of sunlight a day, artificially if necessary. The plant, when outdoors, tolerates light shade, but full sun is best. Plants overwintered indoors will bloom with small blue, purple, white, or pink flowers in late spring to early summer. The small gray-green needle-like leaves are aromatic and add strong flavor to soups, stews, herbal butters, stuffings, breads, meats, fish, and vegetables. The oil is used in toiletries, lotions, soaps, perfumes, and shampoos. The plant can be pruned into a topiary. The flowers are attractive to bees and butterflies, Rutgers rating A.

Rue (ruta graveolens) (ROO-tah grav-ee-OH-lenz)

Rue is a bush native to southeastern Europe and can grow in Zones 4-8 in full sun and medium to dry soil. It reaches three feet in any direction, and the yellow flowers arrive in summer. Plants tolerate some shade as well as drought as long as the soil is well-drained. They don't like wet feet. Prune back in early spring and propagate by seed or cuttings, and add mulch for the winter. Plants have blue-green fern-like leaves that can cause dermatitis when touched. Wear gloves when handling. Leaves are aromatic and toxic if ingested. Rutgers rating A.

Rue, Meadow (thalictrum sp) (thah-LIK-trum)

Meadow Rue consists of separate male and female plants, with the males having the pretty lilac-purple flowers. The bush grows to three feet high and three feet wide, has bluish-green fern-like leaves, and prefers full or partial sun and average well-drained soil. Zones 3-9 and Rutgers rating A.

Sage (salvia officinalis) (SAL-vee-ah oh-fi-shi-NAH-lis)

Sage, also called Culinary Sage or Common Sage, is a staple in the kitchen. It requires full sun and well-drained, dry to medium moisture soils. It can be grown in Zones 3-10 and reaches two and a half feet high and wide. Small lavender-blue flowers arrive in late spring and attract butterflies. It is native to northern Africa and the Mediterranean area and has Rutgers rating A.

Sage, Jerusalem (phlomis fruticosa) (FLOW-miss froo-tih-KOH-suh)

Jerusalem Sage will die to the ground in Zones 5-7, but the roots usually survive. It can only keep itself alive and evergreen in Zones 8-10. The impressive yellow flowers arrive in summer. Deadheading blooms promote a longer blooming season. It prefers medium moisture soils and full sun but can tolerate dry soils and partial sun. It is native to the Mediterranean area, possibly Jerusalem. Rutgers rating A.

Sage, Russian (perovskia atriplicifolia) (per-OV-skee-ah
at-trih-pliss-ih-FOE-lee-ah)

Russian Sage isn't quite Russian at all but originates in the Himalayas and western China. It can grow in Zones 5-9 to a height
of five feet and a width of four feet in full sun and dry to medium,
well-drained soil. The lavender-blue flowers are small but they form
a fragrant blue cloud from July to October. Rutgers rating A. Rabbit-resistant. Cut plants back almost to the ground in late winter or
early spring.

St. John's Wort (hypericum calycinum) (hy-PARE-ih-kum kal-ISS-in-um)

St. John's Wort, sometimes called Creeping St. John's Wort or Aaron's Beard, is a small shrub, growing to a foot high and two feet wide, perfect for a groundcover. It grows well in medium or sandy soils in full sun or partial sun but produces fewer flowers in partial sun. Plant a foot and a half apart as it grows aggressively by underground stems. The upper part of the plant may die in winter, but don't worry. It will grow back in the spring. You should even prune it to three inches above the ground every three years to induce new growth. The yellow flowers cover the plant in summer. Rutgers rating B.

Sassafras (sassafras albidum) (SASS-uh-frass AL-bi-dum)

The Sassafras tree is native to Eastern North America and does well in Zones 4-9 in medium soil and full or part sun. It prefers acidic soil but can tolerate a range of soil types, as long as you don't mind the leaves turning yellow in alkaline soils. It spreads by root suckers, so keep it in check or it will end up looking more like a shrub than a tree. It forms a pyramidal shape about thirty feet tall. The large taproot makes transplanting difficult. Greenish-yellow flowers on female trees produce grape-like clusters in September if pollinated. Excellent red, yellow, and purple fall leaf color. Native Americans used the tree for many culinary uses, and some sources suggest Sassafras tea for preventing breast cancer, but the FDA has recently found carcinogens in the oils, so I wouldn't suggest making any tea.

Savory (satureja montana) (sa-tu-REE-ja mon-TAY-nuh)

Also called Winter Savory, Savory originated in southern Europe and southwestern Asia, and can grow in Zones 5-11 as a perennial herb in full sun and dry to medium soil. Unless you prune it for a formal effect at the edge of a garden, it grows to about a foot tall and one and a half feet wide. The small white flowers arrive in summer, but you should trim back the plants before that, in early spring. The pungent leaves can be used fresh or dried as a seasoning in foods. Rutgers rating B.

Sedge (carex sp) (KARE-eks)

Sedge, sometimes called Yellowfruit Sedge, grows in clumps to three feet tall and two feet wide in moist to wet soils with full sun or partial sun. The leaves look like grass and can be two feet long. The greenish-yellow flowers appear in late spring and ride above the clump on spike-like stems. Zones 4-8.

Sedum (sedum sp) (SEE-dum)

Sedum, commonly known as Moss Stonecrop, is a ground cover that only grows to three inches tall but can spread to cover a two-foot area. Found in Europe, Africa, and Asia in rocky crevices and ravine edges, it can be grown in shallow, rocky, limestone to sandstone, dry to medium soils of moderate to low fertility in full sun or partial sun in Zones 3-10. It spreads fast and tolerates light foot traffic. Tiny yellow flowers appear in summer. Rabbit-resistant.

Serviceberry, Allegheny (amelanchier laevis) (am-uh-LAN-kee-er LAY-viss)

Allegheny Serviceberry trees can be grown in Zones 4-8 in full sun to partial sun. It is tolerant of a wide range of soils but prefers moist, well-drained loams. It usually grows to ten to fifteen feet tall, so can be considered a short tree or tall shrub, depending on who you talk to. White, fairly fragrant, drooping flowers appear in April, followed by berries in June, giving it an alternate name of Juneberry. Native to Eastern North America. The berries are often used in jams, jellies, and pies, and resemble blueberries in appearance and taste. Rutgers rating B.

Smoketree (cotinus coggygria) (ko-TYE-nus kog-GY-gree-uh)

The Smoketree or Smokebush is a shrub native to central Asia and Europe. It grows in Zones 5-8 in full sun. Due to a shallow root system it can't tolerate wet, poorly drained soils. It grows in dry, rocky soil where many other plants have problems. It reaches ten to fifteen feet high and as wide. It gets its name from the billowy hairs which grow on the spent flower clusters. These hairs stay all summer and turn the shrub into a smoky-pink to purplish-pink cloud, and may explain why the deer don't like them very much. I think they tickle their noses. The blue-green leaves turn attractive colors in the fall.

Snapdragons (antirrhinum majus) (an-TEE-ry-num MAY-jus)

Snapdragons are a garden favorite. They come in many varieties: white, yellow, red, orange, peach, purple, and bicolor. You can get varieties that grow to one, two, or three feet tall. They prefer cool summers and can wilt in hot summer months if you're in the southern Midwest. It is winter hardy in Zones 7-10, so most of us will have to buy seedlings every year. If your plants develop rust, plant them in a different area next year. Always buy fungal-resistant seedlings. With deadheading, the blooms can last from April to frost. It requires full sun, and the butterflies and hummingbirds love the flowers. Rutgers rating A.

Snow-in-Summer (cerastium tomentosum) (ker-RAS-tee-um toh-men-TOH-sum)

Snow-in-Summer is a ground cover that spreads rapidly. Plant in areas that are contained, especially in northern areas of the Midwest with full sun and dry, sandy, and well-drained soils. They are winter hardy in Zones 2-10 but dislike the hot summer months in the southern areas. They dislike wet soils and will get root rot. Native to Italy and Sicily, they only grow to a foot high and a foot wide. The white flowers add color to the plants in June. Plants are short-lived, and dead patches may appear after the third year. Rutgers rating B.

Snowdrops (galanthus nivalis) (guh-LAN-thus niv-VAL-us)

Snowdrops grow in Zones 3-7 and are often the first flower to bloom, arriving in February. They are small, only nine inches high and six inches wide. They prefer full sun or partial sun but could be planted under deciduous trees since the trees have no leaves at the time. Plant bulbs two to three inches apart and two to three inches deep in large groups of two dozen or more for the best effect. In ideal conditions, the bulbs will self-seed. Allow the leaves to yellow before removing the bulb from the ground. You don't have to remove the bulb at all if you don't need to replant it elsewhere. It will go dormant once done blooming. Blooms are white and droopy. Rutgers rating A.

Soapwort, Rock (saponaria ocymoides) (sap-oh-NAIR-ee-uh ok-kye-MOY-deez)

Rock Soapwort is a broadleaf evergreen native to the mountains in southern Europe from Spain to the Balkans. It is hardy in Zones 2-9 with pink blooms that go all summer. It prefers dry to medium, well-drained, slightly alkaline soil, and full sun. After flowering, cut back by about half to encourage bushy growth. The clumps reach nine inches high and two feet wide. They don't tolerate foot traffic very well. They can trail and clump, so can be pretty on the edge of a raised garden where the trailing branches can hang over the edge. Stems and leaves are covered with fine hairs, which irritate deer. Rutgers rating B.

Solomon's Seal, Fragrant (polygonatum sp) (pol-ig-on-AY-tum)

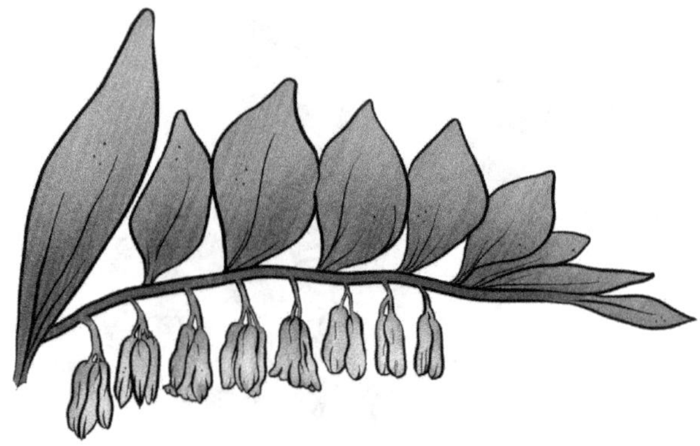

Fragrant Solomon's Seal is a shade-loving perennial that grows to about three feet tall with a foot wide spread. The small, fragrant, white flowers arrive in a line along the stems in late spring, with berries following later. If ingested, any part of this plant will cause discomfort, so don't be tempted to eat the berries. Leave them for the birds. This plant needs medium to wet, well-drained soils in Zones 3-8 with partial sun or shade.

Sourwood (oxydendrum arboreum) (oks-ee-DEN-drum ar-BOR-ee-um)

The Sourwood or Sorrell tree is native to the Eastern US and does best in full sun and acidic soils in Zones 5-9. It pairs well with other acidic soil-loving varities in the Heath family such as azaleas and rhododendrons. It generally grows to thirty feet high by fifteen feet wide and does not do well with drought or urban conditions. Waxy, white flowers arrive in early summer, followed by dry capsules that open to silver-gray in the fall. This gives a pleasant contrast with the crimson red fall coloring of the leaves. The flowers are slightly aromatic; combine that with the gray bark and gray seeds and the deer prefer to pass by. Bees are fond of their flowers and many people are fond of their honey.

Speedwell (veronica sp) (ver-ON-ih-kah)

Speedwell requires full sun and dry to medium moisture soil in Zones 3-11. It reaches six inches tall and nine inches wide, with small blue flowers gracing the scene from May to June. Deadhead blooms after flowering to encourage additional growth. Prune back to basal growth after flowering. Rabbit-resistant. Rutgers rating B.

Spiderwort (tradescantia sp) (trad-es-KAN-tee-uh)

Spiderwort, named for its unattractive habit of spreading like a spiderweb if left alone, grows in Zones 4-11 in partial sun to shade with medium to wet soil. The red, purple, or blue flowers arrive in April. Prune the plant almost to the ground when the flowers are gone, and if the summer is hot, you may get another blooming season in late summer to fall. Divide clumps when they become overcrowded. It reaches two feet high and two feet wide. Rutgers rating B.

Spirea (spiraea sp) (spy-REE-ah)

Spirea bushes are related to roses, as you can see, but in my opinion are easier to maintain. Rated for Zones 4-9, it is grown in full sun in medium soil but tolerates a wide range of soils. Remove old blooms as early as possible to encourage reblooming, pruning a bit if necessary. Prune in late winter or early spring, but only if needed. It will grow to three feet wide and just as tall, and the white or pink blooms are profuse all summer. There are many varieties of Spirea, each with its own individuality. They can be planted in the spring or fall, but there are more available in the springtime.

Spruce, Norway (picea) (PY-see-uh)

Norway Spruce trees grow fast and reach sixty feet tall by thirty feet wide in Zones 2-8. They like their summers cool but sunny as they require full sun. They prefer acidic, rich soils but tolerate sandy soils well and dryish soils once established. They don't flower but produce large cones about nine inches long that hang down from the branches. They're handy as windbreaks, and dwarf varieties are available for gardens.

Spurge   (euphorbia   amygdaloides)   (yew-FOR-bee-ah ah-mig-dah-LOY-deez)

Spurge, also called Wood Spurge, can be found in Zones 6-11. It prefers full sun in the northern areas but likes a little afternoon shade in the south. The yellow flowers arrive in the spring and last quite a while. It needs very well-drained soils as wet soil, especially in the winter, can kill it. It likes dry to medium soils and can tolerate rocky and sandy soil. It grows in an upright mound reaching a foot and a half around. Rabbit-resistant. Wear gloves when handling this plant, as the milky sap can cause skin irritation.

Squill, Siberian (scilla siberica) (SIL-uh sy-BEER-ah-kuh)

Siberian Squill loves northern Minnesota and Michigan's upper peninsula as the seasons remind it of home in Siberia. It is rated for Zones 2-11 with full sun or partial sun. It only gets six inches high, but the blue flowers in spring are beautiful. these bulbs are planted in fall about three inches deep, and they will spread by both bulb offshoots and self-seeding. Plant these around trees and shrubs or in sweeping drifts on slopes or along shady river banks. Rutgers rating A. VERY poisonous when ingested, so don't plant around young children or pets. Can irritate skin in susceptible people.

Star, Blazing (liatris mucronata) (ly-AT-riss muck-ron-AH-tah)

Blazing Star, also called Texas Blazing Star, Narrow-Leaved Gayfeather or Bottlebrush Blazing Star, is native to the southern central US and is winter hardy for Zones 5-9. These plants will reach three feet high and a foot and a half wide. In summer, the purple flowers are used for flower arrangements, if you can ward off the butterflies and bees. The birds like the seeds that come later. It is best grown in medium to dry, sandy to rocky, well-drained soil in full sun. It does not tolerate overly rich soil but does tolerate some drought once established. Rabbit-resistant.

Stocks (matthiola sp) (ma-the-OH-luh)

Stocks, also called Brompton's Stocks, originated in coastal south-ern and western Europe, so is winter hardy only in Zones 7-11. That means we have to buy plants from the nursery in the spring or start them inside from seeds earlier. If you want longer bloom times, sow extra seeds every two weeks. Varieties vary with flower colors of pink, lavender, purple, red, white, and yellow. The flowers are very fragrant, so plant them around windows where you can enjoy them. Generally, they grow to three feet tall with gray-green hairy leaves. Flowers bloom from late spring until frost, but hot humid weather will shorten the bloom time. When grown as a perennial, it develops a woody central stem, which explains Stock's common name. It prefers moist, average to humusy, well-drained soil in full sun. The flowers will wilt if the temperatures stay in the 80s. Rutgers rating B.

Strawberry, Barren (waldsteinia fragarioides) (wald-STINE-ee-uh fray-gare-ee-OY-deez)

Barren Strawberry is native to the eastern US and grows in Zones 3-8 in full sun or partial sun with humusy, slightly acidic soil. Reaching only six inches tall and a foot wide, it is used mostly for a ground cover, as it spreads by underground rhizomes. The yellow spring flowers bloom and are then followed by not strawberries but by inedible seeds. Foliage is evergreen but tends to get bronze in cold climates in the fall.

Strawberry, Wild (fragaria sp) (fray-gare-EE-uh)

Strawberries are fruit-bearing plants that are high-maintenance because of all the diseases they can catch. They are grouped into two: Everbearing, which produces fruit all year long at six-week intervals, and June bearing, producing fruit only once, but having larger berries. Both have white flowers with yellow centers that bloom in spring, followed by delicious berries. Rated for Zones 3-10, they require full sun.

Sumac, Fragrant (rhus aromatica) (roos ar-oh-MAT-ih-kuh)

Fragrant Sumac is a shrub with smaller leaves similar to Poison Sumac, but this plant is not poisonous. The leaves and twigs are aromatic when bruised, giving rise to the name. It grows in Zones 3-9 to a height of six feet and a width of ten feet. The leaves turn attractive colors in the fall. It spreads quickly to form a thicket. The shrubs grow in full sun or partial sun and in a wide range of soils as long as they are well-drained. Tiny yellow flowers bloom in April and give way to berries on the female plant. Sometimes there are both male and female on the same plant, but usually they are separate. Birds love the berries. Rutgers rating A and rabbit-resistant.

Summersweet (clethra alnifolia) (KLEE-thra al-nee-FOH-lee-uh)

Summersweet, also called Sweet Pepperbush, is a popular shrub because it can bloom in partial shade in the late summer. In Zones 3-9, it can grow to eight feet tall by six feet wide in full sun to partial sun and consistently moist, acidic, sandy soils. It prefers partial shade and tolerates clay soils and full shade, but the soil should not be allowed to dry out. The leaves turn nice colors in the fall. The white flowers are aromatic and very attractive to butterflies and bees.

Sunflower, Mexican (tithonia rotundifolia) (ti-THO-nee-a ro-tun-dih-FOH-lee-uh)

Mexican Sunflowers are rated for Zones 2-11, but they love the summer heat. Plant them in full sun and dry to medium soils, although they tolerate poor soils and do not do well in overly rich soil. They appreciate staking when they get high, and they reach six feet tall and three feet wide in a single season. Buy seedlings in the spring. The orange-red with yellow center disks are attractive, and hummingbirds and butterflies love them as they bloom from July to September, and maybe longer if you deadhead the spent blooms.

Sweet-Gum   (liquidambar   styraciflua)   (lih-kwid-AM-bar
sty-rak-ee-FLOO-uh)

The Sweet-Gum tree can be grown in Zones 5-9 in full sun and
medium moisture, well-drained soil. It can tolerate poor soils but not
anything less than full sun. The yellow-green flowers emerge in the
spring and give way to fruit clusters that harden in the fall and stay on
the tree until late winter. Don't plant this tree near a walkway as those
hard clusters can trip you up as they fall during the winter. The sap is
gummy and is used in several applications such as chewing gum, in-
cense, perfumes, folk medicines, and flavorings. The wood is used for
furniture, home interiors, and flooring. The leaves are fragrant when
bruised and turn wonderful colors in the fall. In ideal conditions, this
tree can reach eighty feet tall. Rabbit-resistant.

Sweet-Spire, Virginia (itea virginica) (eye-TEE-uh vir-JIN-ih-kuh)

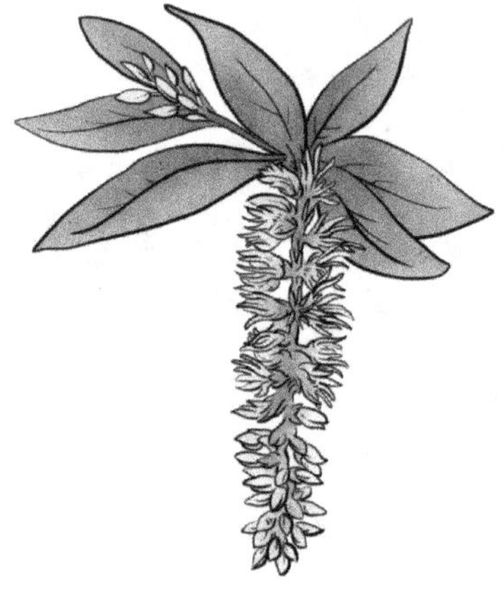

Virginia Sweet-Spire is a native American that grows to five feet tall and five feet wide in Zones 5-9, in full sun or partial sun, and in medium to wet soil. It can form dense colonies by root suckering if left unchecked. White flowers cover the shrub in late spring to early summer. The leaves turn red, orange, and gold shades in fall and often take their time falling to the ground. Rutgers rating B.

Sycamore, American (platanus occidentalis) (PLAT-an-us ok-sih-den-TAY-liss)

The American Sycamore tree is enormous. It can grow to one hundred feet high and one hundred feet wide with a huge trunk measuring up to eight feet across. It is the most massive tree in America and needs a large space. It is also a litterbug, dropping twigs, leaves, fruiting balls, and bark. A sign of a Sycamore you can spot from afar is the exfoliating trunk. The brown bark comes off to reveal the white inner bark. Spring flowers are yellow for males and red for females. Female flowers give way to fruiting balls that eventually burst, dispersing seeds on downy tufts. The wood is used for furniture, crates, barrels, and butcher blocks. Native Americans hollowed out the trunks for canoes. It grows in Zones 4-9 in medium to wet soils in full sun. Also known as Sycamore, Eastern Sycamore, Buttonwood, or Buttonball trees, it can be found in the wild along riverbanks. It will tolerate light shade.

Tarragon (TARE-a-gone) (artemisia dracunculus) (ar-te-MIZ-ee-uh drak-UN-koo-lus)

Tarragon is a perennial shrub that grows in Zones 3-7 in dry to medium soil and full sun. It can reach three feet tall and a foot and a half wide. The yellowish-white flowers come in the summer. Plant it in a sheltered area and mulch it if you want it to survive the winter. Wet soil causes root rot, a known plant killer. Cut the plants to the ground in early spring and divide the plants every three years. Although the leaves are variable in their fragrance and taste, all are used in the kitchen. It is grown in herb gardens and is not considered a good choice for ornamental gardens or borders. Rutgers rating A and rabbit-resistant.

Thistle, Globe (echinops bannaticus) (EK-in-ops ban-AT-ee-kus)

The Globe Thistle is native to southeastern Europe and can be grown in Zones 3-10 in full sun and well-drained soil. It can tolerate poor dry soil as long as it is well-drained. It has a taproot, making it difficult to divide or transplant. The leaves are spiny, as well as the flowers. The gray-blue flowers arrive in the summer. Cut back flowering stems to encourage additional blooms. This plant can reach six feet tall and two feet wide. The flowers make good additions to a cut or dried arrangement. Rabbit-resistant.

Thoroughwort, Tall (eupatorium altissimum)
(yoo-puh-TOR-ee-um al-TISS-ih-mum)

Tall Thoroughwort, also known as Tall Boneset, is a rather weedy perennial herb that grows to six feet tall by three feet wide. In Zones 4-8, with dry to medium moisture, well-drained soils, and full sun or partial sun, it will grow and spread by self-seeding. It will tolerate drought but appreciates some afternoon shade in hot summer climates. The small white flowers are visible from August to October.

Thrift, Sea (armeria maritima) (ar-MER-ee-uh mah-RIT-ih-mah)

Sea Thrift, also known as Sea Pink, will grow where nothing else will, along the sea and in infertile soils. The plant will rot if the soil is too fertile, too moist, or clayish. Good drainage is essential. Rated for Zones 4-8, it only reaches a foot in any direction. The pink to white flowers are pretty in the spring. Rutgers rating B. It requires full sun.

Thyme (TIME) (thymus sp) (TY-mus)

Wild Thyme has many varieties which vary in flavor and aroma. Rated for Zones 4-9, it grows in dry to medium soil in full sun. It tolerates drought and poor soil if the soil is well-drained. It only reaches three inches tall by a foot wide, making it ideal for small areas between footpath stones or along their edges. The deep pink flower comes in August and attracts butterflies with its fragrance. Roots will rot with moist soils or poor drainage. Rutgers rating A.

Toadflax (linaria sp) (lin-AR-ee-uh)

Toadflax plants look like miniature snapdragons. The flowers bloom in spring in many colors and can survive until fall if the summer isn't too hot. Rated for Zones 2-11, they do best as annuals purchased and planted every spring. They reach a foot and a half high and nine inches across and require full sun or partial sun.

Tobacco, Flowering (nicotiana spp) (nih-koe-shee-AY-nah)

The Flowering Tobacco plant is rated for Zones 10-11 so plant it as an annual in the Midwest in moist, well-drained soil in full sun or partial sun. The white flowers look like herald trumpets and arrive in June and stay until the frost. Do not plant these near other members of the Nightshade family (Tomatoes, Peppers, Eggplant, Potato) to avoid transmitting diseases between plants. Also, avoid planting in the same area the next year as other nightshades as the diseases can stay in the soil. The attractive flowers are fragrant and attract hummingbirds and butterflies. In case you were wondering, this variety is not used for making tobacco. Rutgers rating A.

Tree, Chinese Fringe (chionanthus retusus) (kye-oh-NAN-thus re-TOO-sus)

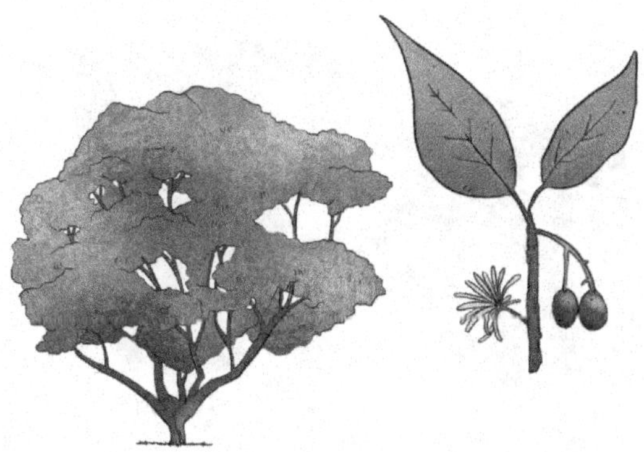

The Chinese Fringe Tree is spectacular in spring when the white flowers bloom. They seem to cover every inch of the tree. It can be grown in Zones 5-9 in medium well-drained soil in full sun or partial sun, although the best flowering occurs with full sun. It can reach twenty feet high with a spread just as large. It prefers acidic soils and can not tolerate prolonged dry conditions. There are separate male and female plants, although they might not be properly labeled. If fertilized, the female flowers give way to olive-like fruits that ripen to bluish-black and feed wildlife during the winter. Leaves turn yellow in the fall. Exfoliating gray-brown bark is attractive in the winter. Rutgers rating B.

Tree, Katsura (cercidiphyllum japonicum) (ser-sid-ih-FIL-um juh-PON-ih-kum)

The Katsura Tree can be grown in Zones 4-8 in rich, moist, well-drained soil in full sun or partial sun. Not tolerant of drought, especially when young, it grows best in an area protected from strong winds and hot afternoon sun. There are separate male and female trees, with slightly different but unimpressive flowers. Clusters of greenish pods follow pollinated flowers on female trees. Leaves turn a spectacular range of red, orange, and gold in the fall, and smell like cinnamon or apples. Trees can reach sixty feet high and just as wide and are good selections for shade trees. Rutgers rating A.

Tree, Tulip (liriodendron tulipifera) (ly-ree-oh-DEN-dron too-lip-EE-fer-uh)

The Tulip Tree, also known as the Yellow Poplar, is the state tree of Indiana, Kentucky, and Tennessee. Its wood is used for furniture, plywood, boatbuilding, paper pulp, and general lumber. Native Americans used the hollowed-out trunks for canoes. The cup-like flowers bloom in the spring and are yellow with an orange band at the base of each petal. Even though the flowers are two inches long, they can often go unnoticed because they arrive after the leaves fully form. Winged seeds follow the flowers. It is best grown in organically rich, well-drained soil in full sun. It will tolerate partial sun. Rated for Zones 4-9, it grows to ninety feet tall with a fifty foot spread. It has impressive fall color and is rabbit-resistant. Rutgers rating B.

Turtlehead (chelone sp) (kay-LOH-nee)

Turtlehead plants are named for the shape of their flowers that bloom from August to October. Rated for Zones 5-8, they can reach four feet high by three feet wide in medium to wet soil and partial sun. If the plant is in full shade, the stems might need staking for support.

Verbena (verbena hybrids) (ver-BEE-nah)

Verbena or Garden Verbena plants, rated for Zones 9-10, are grown as annuals in the Midwest. The profuse flowers bloom from May to October in various colors as long as they have full sun. They are tolerant of heat and drought. Try not to water them from above, but water the ground underneath. Leaves vary from gray-green to dark green. Good choice for window boxes and containers. They reach a foot and a half tall and two feet wide. Butterflies like visiting them.

Vernonia (vernonia sp) (ver-NON-ee-uh)

Vernonia, also called Ironweed, grows to four feet tall by three feet wide in full sun and medium to wet soil in Zones 4-9. The pink or purple flowers last from July to September and attract butterflies. The source of the name Ironweed is somewhat in doubt, but it could be the tough stems, the rusty fringe of the flowers as they fade, or the rusty colored seeds.

Viburnum (viburnum) (vy-BUR-num)

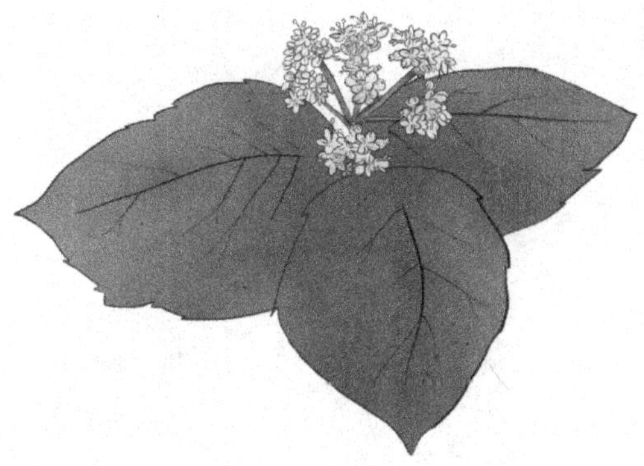

Viburnum is a somewhat early bloomer, arriving in March or April. Plant these in a protected location to prevent losing these flowers to hard freezes. It can be grown in Zones 2-10 in medium moisture, well-drained soils in full sun or partial sun, although you'll get better flowers in full sun. Avoid soils that are either too dry or too wet, as it is a bit picky. The fragrant, tubular flowers bloom on bare stems. These flowers are replaced in late summer by red berries that become blackish in the late fall. The shrub can grow to ten feet high and six feet wide. Plant it where you can enjoy the early fragrant flowers to the utmost. Rutgers rating A. Viburnum opulus teas are considered helpful pain relievers, especially menstrual cramps, according to herbal medicine sources.

Vinca, Annual (catharanthus roseus) (kath-ar-AN-thus ROSE-ee-us)

The range of Annual Vinca, or Madagascar Periwinkle, varies between sources, with one saying Zones 2-11 and another saying 10-11. Since they are annuals and are not expected to survive the winters anyway, I suppose it doesn't matter. They reach only a foot and a half high and as wide with profuse blooms that last from June until the frost. They bloom better in full sun but do fine in partial sun. This flower also dislikes getting its petals wet, so water from underneath. It needs well-drained soil and likes hot humid summer weather. The flower color varies but stays in the pink family. Rutgers rating A and rabbit-resistant.

Violet (viola sp) (vy-OH-lah)

Violets are so lovely when their white flowers, sometimes with a purple tinge, bloom from summer through fall. They self-seed to the point of becoming invasive, so be careful where you plant them. They reach a foot tall and wide and grow in Zones 2-11 in full sun or partial sun in medium to wet, well-drained soil. They can tolerate full shade and like their summers cool, so are ideal choices for northern areas. Rutgers rating B.

Waxbells, Yellow (kirengeshoma palmata) (kih-ren-gesh-OH-mah palm-AY-tah)

Yellow Waxbells are shrubby perennials that grow in Zones 5-8 in partial sun to full shade and moist, acidic, humusy, well-drained soils. They can reach four feet high and three feet wide and produce yellow, waxy, narrow, drooping flowers in early summer, usually in clusters of three that lead to brownish-green three-horned seeds. Rutgers rating B.

Weigela (weigela florida) (wy-GEE-la FLOR-id-uh)

Weigela is a dense shrub that grows to ten feet tall and twelve feet wide in full sun in Zones 4-9. In southern areas, it may appreciate some light dappled shade in the afternoon. The pink flowers explode from April to June, with some sporadic reblooming later. Hummingbirds and humans alike love these flowers. It can tolerate clay soil. Rutgers rating B.

Windflower   (anemone   canadensis)   (ah-NUM-oh-nee
kan-ah-DEN-sis)

Windflower, or Canadian Anemone, is a member of the Buttercup
family, and you can see the family resemblance in the flowers. It is
grown in Zones 3-8 in full sun or partial sun in medium to wet,
well-drained soils. It prefers partial sun and moist, humusy soil, but
appreciates the full sun in cool northern climates. The white flowers
arrive in June on thin hairy stems which sway in the wind, giving way
to the name. They will flop in too much wind or too much shade.
It is tolerant of clay soil. It can spread by creeping rhizomes rather
aggressively.

Wintergreen, Creeping (gaultheria procumbens) (gol-THAIR-ee-uh pro-KUM-benz)

Creeping Wintergreen grows in Zones 3-8 in acidic, well-drained soil in partial sun or shade to a sweeping height of six inches (fooled you) and creeps along the ground. Waxy, nodding, bell-shaped white flowers bloom in early summer, giving way to red berries that persist throughout winter if the birds don't eat them. The leaves smell and taste of Wintergreen, and their oil is used for astringents, diuretics, and stimulants. The flavor is used in toothpaste, chewing gum, and candy. Leaves were once made into poultices for sore muscles and arthritic pain. Fruit is edible and may be eaten raw or added to pastries and salads. The dried leaves have also been used for tea, leading to another name for this plant- Teaberry. Plant these near acid-loving shrubs such as Rhododendrons, Azaleas, Kalmias, and Blueberries. Rutgers rating B.

Wisteria, American (wisteria frutescens) (wis-TEER-ee-ah froo-TESS-enz)

American Wisteria is a climbing vine that can reach forty feet, eventually. Don't expect flowers during the first few years. Prune after reading manuals on the subject. Fertilize the plant after you put it in the soil. It prefers moist, slightly acidic, humusy, well-drained soils and full sun. The purple flowers arrive in May and usually last until June, followed by narrow seed pods that open in the fall. Rated for Zones 4-9.

Witchhazel, Common (hamamelis) (ham-uh-MEE-lis)

Common Witchhazel is a shrub grown in Zones 3-9 in moist, acidic, well-drained soil in full sun to partial sun. The odd-looking, spiky, reddish-purple flowers herald the approach of spring with their arrival in February or March, with the best flowering occurring in full sun. It can tolerate clay soil as long as the drainage is good. The leaves turn a showy yellow in the fall. Root suckers propagate it, so be sure to remove them as you see them. Prune after flowering. It can reach nine feet in height. Rutgers rating B. Witchazel can be used on the skin as an astringent in traditional herbal medicine.

Woodruff, Sweet (galium odoratum)   (GAL-ee-um oh-der-AY-tum)

Sweet Woodruff, also called Sweet Scented Bedstraw, grows in Zones 4-9 with partial sun to shade in medium to wet, well-drained soils. The tiny white flowers bloom in April. This plant can spread aggressively in optimum conditions, but can also go dormant in a drought. Plants emit a scent of freshly mown hay when the leaves are crushed or cut. The leaves are even more aromatic when dried, so they are used in sachets and potpourris. Leaves are also used to make May Wine, a concoction made from white wine, Woodruff, Orange, and Pineapple. Leaves are sometimes used to flavor teas and fruity cold drinks. Rutgers rating A.

Wormwood (artemisia 'povis castle') (ar-te-MEEZ-ee-uh)

Wormwood, rated for Zones 5-8, needs dry to medium, well-drained soils but can grow in poor to moderately fertile soils. It only reaches a foot high by two feet wide, and the yellow flower appears in late summer. Be careful what kind of Wormwood you plant, as some are considered invasive. It likes full sun or partial sun but dislikes wet soil and can get root rot. Rutgers rating A. Rabbit resistant.

Yarrow, Common (achillea millefolium) (uh-KILL-ee-a mill-ee-FOH-lee-um)

Some consider Common Yarrow to be a weed, but some varieties are used for ornamental purposes or for ground cover. They grow to a height of about three feet in Zones 3-10 with full sun and lean, dry to medium, sandy loams. Plants do well in average garden soils as long as the drainage is good. They tolerate hot, humid summers and drought. They tend to flop in those summers and may need staking. The plants have a spicy aroma that persists after drying, making them popular in dried flower arrangements, but not very popular with deer. The white flowers last from June to September and attract butterflies. Rutgers rating B.

Yew,   Japanese   Plum   (cephalotaxus   harringtonia) (sef-uh-loh-TAKS-us har-ring-TOH-nee-uh)

Japanese Plum Yew is a needled evergreen that does well in partial sun and full shade in moist, sandy, well-drained soils. It will tolerate full sun in cool northern summers, but prefers afternoon shade in areas with hot summers. I would plant it in a shady location, as our summers can become hot. Rated for Zones 4-9, it reaches ten feet in any direction but grows slowly. In Zones 4 and 5, plant them in sheltered locations for winter survival. Both male and female plants are needed for fruit production. The fruit resembles plums and is edible. The rest of the plant is toxic, so I'm not sure I would chance the fruit. Rutgers rating A.

Yucca, Spanish Bayonet (yucca variegata)   (YUK-ah var-ee-GAY-tuh)

Yucca (Spanish Bayonet) is a variety of Yucca plant that grows in Zones 4-11 in full sun and dry to medium, well-drained soil. It is tolerant of poor, dry, and sandy soils. It grows to four feet in any direction, with creamy-white flowers arriving in summer, attracting butterflies. This variety has variegated leaves that are blue-green, fading to gold at the edge. Rutgers rating A and rabbit-resistant.

Zinnia (zinnia sp) (ZIN-ee-ah)

Zinnias are ubiquitous in midwestern gardens. Although rated for Zones 2-11, they are planted as annuals each spring and grow to four feet high and two feet across. The varieties have every flower color except blue or brown, which leaves you with many options. The flowers bloom from June to the first frost and attract hummingbirds and butterflies. They make excellent cut flowers. The plants need full sun and humusy, well-drained soils. Rutgers rating B.

Chapter 6

Invasive and Poisonous Plants

Some plants are deer-resistant but are also considered invasive weeds in the Midwest or surrounding areas, so don't even think about planting them. Note that this list includes both Spring and Fall plants. These include:

- Akebia (akebia quinata) (a-KEE-bee-uh kwi-NAY-tuh)

- Sweet Alyssum (lobularia maritima) (lob-yoo-LAR-ee-uh mar-ih-TEE-muh)

- Baby's Breath (gypsophila paniculata) (jip-SOF-il-uh pan-ick-yoo-LAH-tuh)

- Bachelor's Button (centaurea cyanus) (sen-TAR-ee-uh SY-an-us)

- Bamboo, Yellow Grove or Bamboo, Golden (phyllostachys) (fy-lo-STAK-iss)

- Barberry, Japanese (berberis thunbergii) (BUR-bur-is thun-BERG-ee-eye), also called Oregon Grape-Holly (mahonia japonica) (ma-HO-nee-uh juh-PON-ih-kuh)

- Bishop's Weed (aegopodium podagraria) (ee-guh-POH-dee-um pod-uh-GRAR-ee-uh)

- Buckthorn, Common (rhamnus) (RAM-nus)

- Bugloss (anchusa) (an-KOO-suh)

- Catalpa (catalpa) (kuh-TAL-puh)

- Chocolate Vine (akebia) (a-KEE-bee-uh)

- Forget-Me-Not, Woodland (myosotis sylvatica) (my-oh-SO-tis sil-VAT-ee-kuh)

- Grape-Holly, Oregon (mahonia aquifolium) (ma-HO-nee-uh a-kwee-FOH-lee-um)

- Grass, Ribbon (phalaris arundinacea) (FAL-ah-ris a-run-din-uh-SEE-uh), also called Grass, Red Canary

- Not all of the plants in the miscanthus species are invasive, but the only one that is deer-resistant is Grass, Chinese Silver (miscanthus sinensis) (miss-KANTH-us sy-NEN-sis), which is invasive in Indiana.

- Locust, Black Tree (robinia pseudoacacia) (roh-BIN-ee-uh soo-doh-uh-KAY-see-uh)

- Locust, Honey Tree (gleditsia triacanthus) (gleh-DIT-see-uh try-a-KAN-thus)

- Periwinkle (vinca minor) (VIN-kuh MY-nor)

- Many varieties of Privet (ligustrum) (lig-GUS-trum) are invasive, so steer clear of any of them.

- Sunflower, Common (helianthus annuus) (hee-lee-AN-thus AN-yoo-us)

- Valerian (valeriana officianalis) (va-ler-ee-AH-nuh oh-fiss-ih-NAH-liss), also called heliotrope (hee-lee-oh-TROPE)

- Vinca (vinca minor)

- Wisteria, Chinese (wisteria sinensis) (wis-TEER-ee-uh sy-NEN-sis)

- Some varieties of Wormwood (artemisia) (ar-the-MEEZ-ee-uh)

The following have been declared invasive in the southeastern US, so I wouldn't recommend planting them. With global warming, they could easily become invasive in the Midwest.

- Elephant Ears (colocasia esculenta) (kol-oh-KAY-see-uh es-kew-LEN-tuh)

- Japanese Blood Grass (imperata cylindrica) (im-per-AH-tuh sil-IN-dree-kuh)

- Turf Lily (liriope spicata) (lir-RYE-oh-pee spi-KAH-tuh)

These plants have not been declared invasive, but are very aggressive spreaders. Plant them in a contained area or keep an eye on them to prevent them from taking over the yard.

- Aster, False (boltonia asteroides) (bol-TO-nee-uh ass-ter-OY-dees)

- Catnip (nepeta cataria) (NEP-eh-tuh kat-AR-ee-uh)

- Chives, Garlic (allium tuberosum) (AL-ee-um too-ber-OH-sum)

- Comfrey (symphytum rubrum) (sim-FY-tum ROO-brum)

- Creeper, Trumpet (campsis radicans) (KAMP-sis RAD-ee-kans)

- Foxglove (digitalis purpurea) (dij-ee-TAH-liss pur-PUR-ee-uh)

- Goldenrod (solidago hybrids) (so-li-DAY-go)

- Horehound (marrubium vulgare) (ma-ROO-bee-um vul-GAIR-ee)

- Horseradish (armoracia rusticana) (ar-mor-AY-shee-uh rus-tik-AH-nuh)

- Jacob's Ladder (polemonium caeruleum) (po-le-MOH-nee-um see-ROO-lee-um)

- Lady's Mantle (alchemilla mollis) (al-kem-ILL-uh MAW-liss)

- Mint, Mountain (pycanthemum pilosum)

(pik-NAN-thee-mum pil-OH-sum)

- Morning Glory (ipomea sp) (ip-oh-MEE-a)

- Mullein (verbascum sp) (ver-BASK-um)

- Pennyroyal (mentha pulegium) (Men-thuh pul-ee-GEE-um)

- Plant, Obedient (physostegia virginiana) (fy-so-STEG-ee-uh vir-jin-ee-AN-uh)

- Poppy, Plume (macleaya cordata) (ma-KLAY-uh kor-DAY-tuh)

- St. John's Wort (hypericum calycinum) (hy-PER-ee-kum ka-LEE-kin-um)

- Snow-in-Summer (cerastium tomentosum) (ker-RAS-tee-um toh-men-TOH-sum)

- Violet (viola sp) (vee-OH-la)

- Windflower (anemone canadensis) (uh-NEM-oh-nee ka-na-DEN-sis)

- Woodruff, Sweet (galium odoratum) (GAL-ee-um oh-dor-AH-tum)

The following are poisonous to ingest, so don't plant these around pets or young children. Note that this list includes both Spring and Fall plants.

- Bloodroot (sanguinaria canadensis) (san-gwin-AR-ee-uh

ka-na-DEN-sis)

- Bush, Lily of the Valley (pieris japonica) (pee-AIR-iss juh-PON-ih-kuh) leaves and flowers

- Coralberry "Snowberry" (symphoricarpos albus) (sim-for-ee-KAR-poss AL-bus)

- Creeper, Trumpet (campsis radicans)KAMP-sis RAD-ee-kans) honorable mention for itchiness from skin contact

- Devil's Walking Stick (aralia spinosa) (uh-RAY-lee-uh spy-NO-suh) bark can irritate skin

- Four O'Clock (mirabilis jalapa) (mih-RAB-ih-liss juh-LAP-a)

- Foxglove (digitalis purpurea) (dij-ee-TAH-liss pur-PUR-ee-uh) leaves

- Gas Plant (dictamnus alba) (dik-TAM-nus AL-ba) honorable mention for allergic reactions from contact with oil

- Jack-in-the-Pulpit (arisaema triphyllum) (air-uh-SEE-muh try-FIL-um) roots

- Larkspur (consolida ambigua) (kon-SO-lih-duh am-BIG-yoo-uh) leaves, flowers, roots if ingested

- Monkshood (aconitum) (a-kon-EYE-tum) ingestion or even touch is dangerous

- Rhubarb (rheum) (REE-um) leaves

- Rose, Christmas or Lenten (helleborus nigra) (hell-eh-BORE-us NY-gruh)

- Rue (ruta graveolens) (ROO-tuh grav-ee-OH-lens) leaves

- Sassafras (sassafras albidium) (SASS-uh-frass AL-bi-dum) carcinogenic oil

- Solomon's Seal, Fragrant (polygonatum) (po-lig-oh-NAY-tum)

- Spurge (euphorbia amygdaloides) (yoo-FOR-bee-uh am-ig-duh-LOY-deez) honorable mention for sap's skin irritation

- Squill, Siberian (scilla siberica) (SKI-uh sy-BEER-ah-kuh)

- Yew, Japanese Plum (cephalotaxus harringtonia) (se-uh-loh-TAKS-us har-ring-TOH-nee-uh) The berries are edible but the rest is toxic.

Chapter 7

Bonus Section: Rabbit-Resistant Plants

These plants are deer-resistant, of course, but also rabbit-resistant. Detailed notes are above, so you will find only their common and Latin names listed here.

- Ageratum (ageratum houstonianum)

- Aster, Stokes (stokesia laevis)

- Astilbe (astilbe sp)

- Barrenwort (epimedium x perralchicum)

- Basil (ocimum basilicum)

- Bee Balm (monarda didyma)

- Bleeding Heart (dicentra sp)

- Bluebell, Virginia (mertensia virginica)

- Boxwood (buxus sempervirens)

- Brunnera, Heartleaf (brunnera macrophylla)

- Bunchberry (cormus canadensis)

- Bush, Butterfly (buddleia davidii)

- Candytuft (iberis sempervirens)

- Cotoneaster (cotoneaster)

- Cotoneaster Bearberry (cotoneaster dammeri)

- Crocosmia (crocosmia sp)

- Crown Imperial (fritillaria imperialis 'lutea')

- Daffodil (narcissus)

- Daisy, Shasta (leucanthermum x superbum)

- Delphinium (delphinium sp)

- Dogwood, Flowering (cornus)

- Fern, Christmas (polystichum acrostichoides)

- Fern, Cinnamon (osmunda cinnamonea)

- Fern, Sensitive (onoclea sensibilis)

- Foamflower (tiarella cordifolia)

- Four O'Clock (mirabilis jalapa)

- Geranium (geranium sp)

- Germander (teucrium chamaedrys)

- Grape (vitis coignetiae)

- Horehound (marrubium vulgare)

- Hyacinth (hyacinthus)

- Lady's Mantle (alchemilla mollis)

- Lamb's Ears (stachys byzantina)

- Laurel, Mountain (kalmia)

- Lavender (lavandula augustifolia)

- Lilac, Common (syringa vulgaris)

- Lily, Turf (lirope spicata)

- Lupine (lupinus sp)

- Maple, Full Moon (acer japonicum o-isami)

- Monkshood (aconitum sp)

- Pachysandra (pachysandra terminalis)

- Plant, Ice, Creeping Shrubby (ruschia pulvinaris)

- Poker, Red Hot (kniphoflia tritoma)

- Rhododendron (rhododendron)

- Rhubarb (rheum hybrids)

- Sage, Russian (perovskia atriplicifolia)

- Sedum (sedum sp)

- Speedwell (veronica sp)

- Spurge (euphorbia amygdaloides)

- Star, Blazing (liatris mucronata)

- Sumac, Fragrant (rhus aromatica)

- Sweet-Gum (liquidambar styraciflua)

- Tarragon (artemisia dracunculus)

- Thistle, Globe (achinps bannaticus)

- Tree, Tulip (liriodendron tulipifera)

- Vinca Annual (catharanthus roseus)

- Wormwood (artemisia 'povis castle')

- Yucca, Spanish Bayonet (yucca gloriosa 'variegata')

Definitions

Annual: living only one growing season, as beans or corn.

Biennial: completing its normal term of life in two years, flowering and fruiting the second year, as beets or winter wheat.

Bulb: 1) a usually subterranean and often globular bud having fleshy leaves emergent at the top and a stem reduced to a flat disk, rooting from the underside, as in the onion and lily; 2) a plant growing from such a bud.

Ground Cover: 1) the herbaceous plants and low shrubs in a forest, considered as a whole; 2) any of a variety of low-growing or trailing plants used to cover the ground in areas where grass is difficult to grow, as in dense shade or on steep slopes.

Hardy: able to withstand the cold of winter in the open air.

Herb: a flowering plant whose stem above ground does not become woody, especially if such a plant when valued for its medicinal properties, flavor, scent, or the like.

Perennial: a plant having a life cycle of more than two years.

Shrub: a woody plant smaller than a tree, usually having multiple permanent stems branching from or near the ground.

Tree: a woody perennial plant, typically having a single stem or trunk growing to a considerable height and bearing lateral branches at some distance from the ground:

Vine: 1) any plant having a long, slender stem that trails or creeps on the ground or climbs by winding itself about a support or holding fast with tendrils or claspers; 2) the stem of any such plant.

References

Better Homes and Gardens http://www.bhg.com/gardening/plant -dictionary

Curtis, Paul D., Cornell Cooperative Extension Monroe County and Richmond, Milo E., New York Cooperative Fish and Wildlife Research Unit. Reducing Deer Damage to Ornamental and Garden Plants. (2018) http://cce.cornell.edu/monroe

"Deer-resistant Trees and Shrubs for Iowa," http://www.theiowa gardener.com

Fast Growing Trees https://www.fast-growing-trees.com/collecti ons/deer-resistant

Finnegran, Rebecca. Winter deer damage heavy? Seek deer-resistant plants. (2015) Michigan State University http://www.msu.edu
Gurneys http://www.gurneys.com

Indiana deer-resistant plants and repellants Indiana University h ttp://www.iun.edu

http://www.deerfriendly.com/deer.indiana-deer-resistant-plants-and-repellents

Missouri Botanical Garden http://www.missouribotanicalgarden.org/PlantFinder

Nuisance Wildlife Repellent Handbook. Minnesota Department of Natural Resources, Wildlife Damage Management Program

Plants not Favored by Deer. The Morton Arboretum, https://mortonarb.org/plant-and-protect/tree-plant-care/plant-care-resources/plants-not-favored-by-deer/

Nuisance Wildlife Repellent Handbook. Minnesota Department of Natural Resources, Wildlife Damage Management Program

Rutgers http://www.njaes.rutgers.edu/deer-resistant-plants

Spring Hill Nursery www.springhillnursery.com

The Top Deer-Resistant Plants for the Midwest. (2016) https://bhg.com/gardening/gardening-by-region/midwest/the-top-deer-resistant-plants-for-the-midwest

University of Illinois, Extension https://web.extension.illinois.edu/perennials/specific

http://www.extension.illinois.edu/blogs/good-growing/2018-05-17-oh-deer

University of Minnesota, Extension http://www.extension.umn.edu/yard-and-garden

https://extension.umn.edu/planting-and-growing-guides/white-tailed-deer-damage

USDA Plant Hardiness Zone Map https://planthardiness.ars.usda.gov/pages/view-maps

Links to Useful Sites

Look at the interactive USDA Zone map here:

https://planthardiness.ars.usda.gov/pages/view-maps

These links to sunrise times, sunset times, and day length may come in handy when you're deciding when to bring those plants inside for the winter.

https://sunrise-sunset.org/calendar

https://www.suntoday.org/sunrise-sunset/2021.html

This site tells you how to pronounce Latin names:
http://www.davesgarden.com/botanary

Acknowledgements

I would like to thank my friend (of almost sixty years!) Mary Golden for her emotional support and proofreading. I would also like to thank my sister Lorna Allard and my friend Terri Pattio for their encouragement.

Also by Sue Monson

Deer-Resistant Gardening in the Midwest: Spring Planting Edition, Sue Monson, Almennigen Enterprises, 2022.

Deer-Resistant Gardening in the Midwest: Fall Planting Edition, Sue Monson, Almennnigen Enterprises, 2023.